1 MONTH OF
FREE
READING

at

www.ForgottenBooks.com

By purchasing this book you are eligible for one month membership to ForgottenBooks.com, giving you unlimited access to our entire collection of over 1,000,000 titles via our web site and mobile apps.

To claim your free month visit:

www.forgottenbooks.com/free907975

ISBN 978-0-266-90767-1
PIBN 10907975

FRUIT AND ORNAMENTAL
TREES AND PLANTS,
BULBOUS FLOWER ROOTS,
GREEN-HOUSE PLANTS, &c. &c.

CULTIVATED AT THE

LINNÆAN BOTANIC GARDEN,

WILLIAM PRINCE, *Proprietor,*

Flushing, Long-Island, near New-York.

TO WHICH IS ADDED,

A SHORT TREATISE
ON THEIR CULTIVATION, &c.

———◆———

" *A wood coeval with himself he sees,*
" *And loves his own cotemporary trees.*"

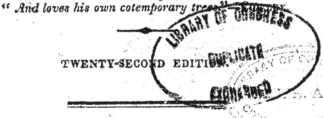

TWENTY-SECOND EDITION.

NEW-YORK:
PRINTED BY T. AND J. SWORDS,
No. 99 Pearl-street.

———

1823.

|2 |3 |4

PREFACE.

THE LINNÆAN GARDEN was commenced about the middle of the last century, by WILLIAM PRINCE, the father of the present proprietor, at a time when there were few or no establishments of the kind in this country. It originated from his rearing a few trees, to ornament his own grounds; but finding, after the first efforts had been attended with success, that he could devote a portion of his lands more lucratively to their cultivation for sale, than to other purposes, he commenced their culture more extensively, and shortly after published a Catalogue which, at that early period, contained several hundred species and varieties, and hence arose the first extensive fruit collection in America. At that time the study of Botany received but little attention in our country, and the labours of the great Linnæus had not yet shone upon the world, although his diligent researches in the great field of science were not unknown to the favoured few who were honoured with his correspondence. Almost the only aid, therefore, which the founder of this garden possessed, to enable him to develope the great Book of Nature, was derived from his own persevering genius and assiduity.

Practical horticulture being at that day quite a novelty in America, his garden early attracted the notice of persons of taste and science, and from it were disseminated throughout Europe, at a very early period, a large number of the vegetable productions of the western world. The Sound, or East River, about eight miles above the city of New-York, throws an arm into Long-Island, to the distance of six miles, and forms what is denominated "Flushing Bay." At the head of this beautiful Bay lies a wide expanse of luxuriant marine meadows, around which rises an amphitheatre of gently undulating hills. On one of these gentle declivities stands the village of Flushing, and here the LINNÆAN GARDEN is situated, at a distance of but twelve miles from the Ocean, three from the Sound, or East River, and ten from the city of New-York—between which and the village two stages and a steam-boat go and return daily, affording conveyances the most convenient and pleasurable to such citizens as delight in a rural retreat during the verdant season. The venerable founder, after having acquired for his garden an extensive fame, died in the year 1802, at an advanced age, leaving his son, the present proprietor, in the possession of his collection; who has, at a great expense, imported from almost every country in Europe, and also from Asia and Africa, such trees and plants as were best calculated to improve and ornament the Orchard, the Garden, and the Green-house.

The immense losses which have frequently occurred by plants rotting and dying on the voyage of importation, have caused the disbursements in this way to be very great; the same plant has, in some instances, been imported the twentieth time before it survived, and thousands of dollars have been expended in importations and experiments, from which no pecuniary benefits have been derived. It has also been necessary to import a very extensive variety, in order to make the proper selection of those kinds which were most congenial to our climate; and the present collection of fruits is the result of much investigation, and is selected from a very large number, a portion of which had to be rejected on account of their indifference in quality, the small quantity they yielded, or their unsuitableness to our climate. It is, therefore, not without great exertions, attended with an immense expense, that the collection has been increased to above 4,000 species and varieties, many of which, from being objects of curiosity alone, or held in esteem only as they regard science, yield no remuneration.

As medical practice is so nearly connected with the science of Botany, it is the desire of the proprietor to add to the establishment all exotics which have been celebrated for their medicinal properties; and arrangements have been made, which will greatly extend that part of the collection, and by far the greater number of those which are natives of our own country, and whose medicinal virtues have been established by the investigations of Drs. Bigelow and Barton, and which have been figured in their respective publications, will already be found in the collection. It has also been an object of particular consideration, to extend as much as possible the number of the Indigenous Vegetable productions of our own country generally; but, in a country so extensive as our's, and where so few gentlemen of Botanic science are found in its remoter regions, these exertions, although crowned with much success, have also been necessarily attended with very great, and, in some cases, almost discouraging difficulties. Thomas Nuttall, Esq. a gentleman celebrated as much for the liberality of his mind as for his great attainments in Botany, and other sciences, presented me with seeds of all the species collected during his western tour—a very considerable number of which have flowered, and are now in a thriving state. During the recent Yellow Stone expedition, under Col. Long, Dr. James also made a collection of seeds of eighty-four species on the Rocky Mountains, and elsewhere; which he very politely presented to this establishment, and among which it is expected will be found not only a large number of new species, but also some new genera.

At the period at which this garden was commenced, few of the finer fruits of Europe had yet found their way to America, and no person had yet paid any attention to the amelioration or improvement of such as our own country afforded; but, at the present time, we have not only by far the greater part of the most celebrated fruits of Europe and Asia, but can also boast the origin of many which rival those of the old world, and which are sought after with avidity by the inhabitants of the eastern hemisphere, and are considered by them as valuable acquisitions to their already great collections; and, that our country is every way equal to others in the improvement and perpetuity of fruits, is a truth no longer doubted.

It has been thought adviseable to add to the Catalogue a short but general Treatise on cultivation, as it will be of service to those who do not already possess general information on the subject, or who have not within their reach the benefit of more copious publications. The culture of Bulbous Flowers, which have heretofore received but little attention in this country, has also been dwelt upon, from a positive conviction, that no climate is more congenial to the developement of their transcendent beauties than the middle states of the Union, which possess all the advantages of Holland, with none of the disadvantages which they so much deprecate as appertaining to their climate. In the nomenclature of the trees and plants, I have taken for a guide the generally approved names of Linnæus, and, for those of more recent discovery, I have been guided by Wildenow, Michaux, Pursh, and some other authors of acknowledged celebrity; and, for the gratification of scientific horticulturists, I have annexed the French names to such fruits as were originally imported from France.

The extent of the garden is at present about twenty acres, the whole of which is exclusively devoted to the cultivation of trees and plants; and the Green and Hot-houses form a front of 100 feet, with a depth of 30 feet; and it is purposed to enlarge both the garden and the buildings, as the increasing demand for the objects to which they are devoted may render it necessary.

Very large accessions are making monthly to the Greenhouse collection, and also to the establishment generally, as well by extensive importations from the most celebrated collections of Europe, as by the interchange of civilities with Botanic Gardens in different quarters of the globe, and the liberal contributions of gentlemen of science and research, whose pleasure or avocations call them to remote regions; and seeds of several hundred very valuable species are now in the possession of the proprietor, which have been received from these sources, but which it is contrary to the rules of this establishment to publish as in their possession, until their culture shall have been crowned with success. The frequent intercourse now established between this country and China has also induced the proprietor to make direct importations from that country, which perhaps is more rich in splendid flowers than any other known, and the success of these efforts have been hitherto such as to encourage their continuance.

It, therefore, may confidently be hoped, that ere long our country will possess a Botanic collection, at least equal to many of those which have received the patronage of the governments of Europe; and it is but reasonable that an empire, extending from the Atlantic to the Pacific Ocean, and embracing in its latitudinal dimensions every climate of the earth, and whose Flora, no doubt, co-extensive with its variety of climes and soils, must form a very large division of the vegetable kingdom, should possess a Botanic collection superior to those of the diminutive countries of Europe, and which should concentrate at least all the plants indigenous to our own; and it is here perhaps to be regretted, that the munificence of our government has not been directed to the accomplishment of such an object, by the establishment of a National Botanic Institution founded on this principle at the city of Washington, both its climate and situation being peculiarly favourable to such an undertaking.

I cannot conclude my prefatory remarks without acknowledging my obligations to a number of gentlemen for their polite contributions to this establishment, especially to Professor Thouin, Administrator of the Royal Gardens at Paris; Thomas Nuttall, Esq. author of the " Genera of American Plants;"

Cambridge University; the Hon. Jonathan Hunewell, of Boston; Dr. Porter, of Plainfield; John Champneys, and N. Herbemont, Esqrs. of South-Carolina; Mrs. Louisa C. Shaw, Capt. John Le Conte, John Cooper, John Watkins, and Thomas Young, Esqrs. of Georgia; Dr. Hart, of Natchez; D. Reinhardt, and John D. Beatty, Esqrs. of North-Carolina; Dr. Norton, and Dr. Hening, of Richmond; Dr. Thornton, of Washington; the Rev. Mr. Heckewelder, of Pennsylvania; Dr. Hulings, of Philadelphia; Dr. James, of Albany; Dr. David Hosack, Professor Mitchell, the Rev. Mr. Schaeffer, and Dr. Torrey, of New-York—from all whom seeds or plants have been received, which it would perhaps have been impossible to have obtained from other sources.

CURSORY REMARKS.

THE Fruit Trees in this Catalogue are either grafted or inoculated, and are propagated from such European and American kinds as have acquired a well merited celebrity; the selection of which has been made with care and attention. Every precaution is taken which is necessary to preserve the different varieties perfectly distinct, and all the Peach and other trees are perfectly healthy, and free from disease.

It may also be well to observe, that some of the fruits particularized in this Catalogue, and which are of *European* origin, differ from those of the same name described in Mr. Cox's work on Fruit Trees, which are of *American* origin, as names taken from English publications have sometimes been given to fruits originating in America, which differ both in form and flavour from the European kinds; therefore, where it is desirable to have the particular kinds described in that work, it will be necessary that the order should specify it.

Every tree, when sent from the garden, is duly labelled; and from fifteen to twenty-five trees are usually packed in each matted bundle.

Where trees are requested for exportation, they are carefully packed in matts, casks, or boxes, so as to be sent to Europe, the West-Indies, or any part of America, with perfect safety.

All packages of trees are delivered at Fulton-market wharf, New-York, by water, *free of freight;* and, when particularly desired by persons at a distance, they will be shipped to any port they may designate; and agreements have been made with the lines of packets to Boston, Baltimore, Washington, Richmond, Charleston, and Savannah, to take the bundles of trees at very moderate freights.

American Indigenous Trees, Shrubs, and Plants, or their Seeds, suitable for sending to Europe, (of which Catalogues are published distinct from the present,) will be supplied in assortments from $5 to $500.

Scions of the various Fruit Trees for ingrafting, packed in the most portable and secure manner, will be furnished at fifty cents per dozen, but no less than a dozen of any kind can be supplied.

The prices for trees, &c. are, by mutual agreement, the same with other establishments in the vicinity. Trees of extra large size will be charged in proportion.

The proper seasons for transplanting trees are the months of October, November, and December, in autumn; and March and April, in the spring. For Bulbous Flower Roots, the best season is from July to October inclusive. Green-house Plants can be forwarded with safety at any season, except the winter months.

It seems almost superfluous to remark, that all trees and plants in this Catalogue, not particularly designated as tender, are hardy.

Catalogues may be obtained gratis of either of the agents, and orders left with them, or forwarded (post paid) to the proprietor, will meet attention; but it is expected that persons forwarding orders otherwise than through an agent, will designate some person in New-York, who will be responsible for the payment.

As a prejudice has prevailed from time immemorial, that trees, like cattle, when removed from a rich to a poorer soil cannot thrive, and as nursery grounds are generally supposed to be kept in the richest possible state, it is a duty which the proprietor of this establishment owes to himself to state, that for many years he has not made use of as much manure on his grounds as is commonly put on the same quantity of ground by farmers in their usual course of agriculture—not from any belief in the above mentioned doctrine, but from motives of economy, resulting from actual experiment, he has substituted culture for manure, by having his grounds, previously to planting, ploughed more than twice the usual depth, and by having the ground each year dug along side of the rows of trees. By this management they are continued in the most thrifty state until the period for transplantation. The doctrine of trees not thriving when removed from rich to poorer soil has long since been exploded in Europe. Marshall, a celebrated English writer, is very particular on this subject, and gives instances that have come under his observation to prove its fallacy, in his " Rural Economy of the Midland Counties of England," vol. i. p. 85. It is absolutely necessary the young trees, at the time of transplanting, should be vigorous and thrifty, and it is of no consequence whether this is produced by strength of soil or by culture, as the young tree will then have a constitution prepared to feed itself on coarser food.

N. B. It is expected that no persons having similar establishments will copy the Treatise, or other remarks attached to this Catalogue, without crediting the source, as it would be extremely unreasonable that other persons should take upon themselves the responsibility for any errors which may have been inadvertently advanced by the author of this publication.

INDEX.

———

APPLES, 37½ Cents. Pyrus *malus.*
Class, *Icosandria.* Order, *Pentagynia.*

[In the arrangement of the Apples I have thought best to place those which are peculiarly adapted for Cider in a separate division—there is but little doubt, however, that many of those kinds, now more particularly esteemed for the Table, may, on trial, prove extremely good for Cider also; where such trials have already proved successful, it is designated.]

TABLE FRUIT.

C denotes those which have proved good for Cider also.
P ——— those which are proper for preserving or cooking.
O ——— those which are ornamental only.

B

1 YELLOW harvest, *the earliest of apples, fit for tarts in June, and an excellent table fruit* ripe in July.

2 Sine qua non   do

3 White juneating   do

4 Red juneating   do

5 Large early bough   August.

6 Summer rose, P   do

7 Summer queen, P   do

8 Summer pearmain, P   do

9 Red calville, *calville rouge d'été*   do

10 Dwarf paradise   do

11 Marygold   do

12 Red and green sweeting, *weighs a pound*   Aug. & Sept.

13 English codlin, P   do

14 Maiden's blush, P   do

15 Large white sweeting   September.

16 Quince   do

17 Siberian crab, *Pyrus prunifolia. This fruit, which is crimson and yellow, is peculiarly beautiful,* P   do

18 Cherry crab, *Pyrus baccata,* P   do

19 Double blossom Chinese, *Pyrus spectabilis, with clusters of flowers like roses,* O 50 cents   do

20 Scarlet flowering Japan, *Pyrus japonica,* O $1   do

21 Loan's pearmain   September and October.

22 Rambo, *or Romanite,* P   do

23 Autumn bough   do

24 Red bough   do

25 Transparent, *pomme transparente, or pomme de glace*   do

26 Gros drap d'or   September to November.

27 Fall pippin, *weighs a pound*   do

28 Corlies' sweeting, C   September to December.

29 Aromatic russet   October and November.

30 Fama gusta, *from Cyprus*   do

31 Autumn pearmain   do

32 English wine   do

33 American nonpareil, *doctor apple*   do

34 Monstrous bellflower   do

35 Hawthorndean   October to January.

36 Catline, *of Maryland,* C   do

37 Pear shaped   do

38 Newtown Spitzenburgh   do

39 Rose, *pomme de rose, or gros api*   do

40 Monstrous pippin, *ox apple, or New-York gloria mundi, has weighed 27 to 35 oz.* P   do

47 Golden reinette, *reinette doré*, C   do
48 French red reinette   November to March.
49 Long-Island russet   do
50 Ruckman's pearmain, C   do
51 Federal pearmain   do
52 Golden pearmain, C   do
53 Royal pearmain, C   do
54 Winter sweet pearmain   do
55 Reinette-grise   do
56 Belden, *or red cheek*   do
57 Queen's apple   do
58 Red Baldwin pippin   do
59 Red jellyflower   do
60 Lemon pippin   do
61 Margill   do
62 Surprise, *yellow outside, and red to the core within*   do
63 English nonpareil   do
64 Seek-no-farther   do
65 Royal russet, *or leather coat*, P   do
66 White calville, *calville blanche d'hyver*, P   do
67 Æsopus Spitzenburgh, *thought by many inferior to none*   do
68 Flushing Spitzenburgh   do
69 Lady apple, *pomme d'api, greatly admired*   do
70 Red Winter sweeting   do
71 Yellow bellflower   do
72 Black, *pomme noire*   do
73 Vandervere, P   do
74 Dickskill   do
75 Swaar   do
76 Craam   do
77 Pomme gris, *grey apple*   do
78 English Wine   do
79 Red spice, *fenouillet rouge, bardin, or pomme d'anis*   do
80 Yellow spice, *fenouillet jaune, or petit drap d'or*   do
81 Winter queening, *of Ohio*   November to March.
82 Lady's finger   November to April.
83 Ribston pippin, P   do
84 Rhode-Island greening, *weighs a pound*   do

85 Jersey greening   *ripe from* November to June.
86 English golden pippin   do
87 Priestly, P   December to April.
88 Moore's sweeting
89 Green everlasting   } *These apples have been pre-*
90 Red everlasting   *served sound above a year,*
91 Boston russeting, *Rox-*   December to June.
   bury russeting
92 Green Newtown pippin. *This apple is considered un-*
   rivalled; none stands higher as a table fruit, and no
   cider is superior to what is made of it, when the
   fruit is well ripened, C   do
93 Yellow Newtown pippin, C P   do
94 Carthouse, *or Gilpin,* C   January to May.
95 Redling   do
96 Tewksbury blush   January to July.

CIDER APPLES.

T denotes those that are good table fruit also.
P ———— those that are best for preserving.

97 Wetherill's white sweeting, T   *ripe in* September.
98 Poveshon   September and October.
99 Hagloe crab, P   September to November.
100 Greyhouse, T   October and November.
101 Fort Magee crab, P   do
102 Sweet scented crab, P   do
103 Hughes' Virginia crab   do
104 Gloucester white, *of Virginia,* T   do
105 Cann   do
106 Graniwinkle   do
107 Roane's white crab   October to January.
108 Styre   do
109 Winesap, T   do
110 Campfield, *or Newark sweeting*   do
111 Pumpkin sweeting   October to February.
112 Herefordshire red streak, P   November to February.
113 Cooper's russeting, T P   November to March.
114 Harrison's Newark   do

Select kinds of Apples are propagated on Paradise stocks for
   Dwarfs or Espaliers.

PEARS, 37½ Cents. Pyrus *communis*.
Class, *Icosandria*. Order, *Pentagynia*.

[The varieties of Pears are so numerous, that the European and American
kinds together would form a list of several hundreds. A succession of
the best kinds, or what is termed in France the *Circle of Pears*, affording the best sorts for the table, and for culinary purposes, throughout the
year, may be selected from the following, which are of the most approved
kinds.]

      M denotes melting pears.
      B ———— baking or preserving pears.
      P ———— perry pears.

1 Primitive	*ripe in* July
2 Supreme, *little musk, or petit muscat*	do
3 Early sugar	do
4 Green chisel, *citron de carmes, or madeleine*, M	do
5 Red muscadelle, *twice bearing*, M	do
6 Summer beauty, *or bellissme d'été*	do
7 Sugartop, *July, or harvest*	do
8 Petit muscat, *sept en gueule, or early cluster*	do
9 Jargonelle, M	August.
10 Cuisse madame	
11 Skinless, *early rousselette, poire sans peau, or fleur de Guignes*, M	do
12 Avorat, *August muscat, or poire royale*, M	do
13 Fondante d'été, *summer melting*, M	do
14 Windsor, M	do
15 Summer rousselette, *gros rousselette, or roi d'été*	do
16 Late green chisel, M	do
17 Gross blanquet, *or mussette d'Anjou*, M	do
18 Muscat robert, *muscat d'ambre, or poire à la reine*	do
19 Early Catharine, *rousselet hatif*	do
20 Musk summer bon chretien, *bell pear, or bon chretien d'été musqué*, M	do
21 Summer bergamot, *bergamotte d'été, or Milan*, M	do
22 Two headed, *deux têtes*	do
23 Crawford	do
24 Aurate	do
25 Epargne, *beau present, or St. Samson*, M	do
26 Julienne, *archduc d'été, or summer beurré*	do
27 Red bergamot, *bergamotte rouge or crasanne d'été*	do
28 Salviati	September.
29 Ognonet, *or brown admired*	do
30 Autumn golden russet	do

31 Royal summer, *royale d'été*   *ripe in* September.
32 Perfumed, *parfum d'aout*   do
33 Mouille bouche, *verte longue,* or *great mouth water,* M do
34 Striped dean, *verte longue panachée,* or *culotte de Suisse*   do
35 Rousselette de Rheims, *petit rousselet, musk,* or *spice,* M   do
36 Brown Beurré, *beurré grise,* M   do
37 Golden Beurré, *beurré doré,* M   do
38 Bloody, *la sanguinole,* B   do
39 Cassolette, *or muscat vert*   do
40 Orange bergamot, B   do
41 Lowree's bergamot, M   do
42 Autumn bergamot, M   do
43 Broca's bergamot, M   do
44 Gansel's bergamot, M   do
45 Rosewater, *caillot rosat*   do
46 Rockland   do
47 Buffum's, M   do
48 Washington, M   September and October.
49 Virgalieu, *Doyenné, St. Michel, Dean's pear, beurré blanc,* or *garner,* M   do
50 Pope's scarlet major   do
51 Pope's Quaker   do
52 Crasanne bergamot   October.
53 Bergamot sylvanche   do
54 White and Grey Messire Jean   do
55 Poir de prince, *or the prince's pear*   do
56 Brest melting, *fondante de Brest,* M   do
57 Seckle, *by many thought superior to all others,* M   do
58 Doyenné gris, *late virgalieu,* M   do
59 Prince's virgalieu, M   do
60 Red muscat, *muscat rouge*   do
61 Autumn bon chretien, *bon chretien d'automne*   do
62 Autumn bounty, M   do
63 Woolly, or *sage leaved, Pyrus pollveria, ornamental only.*   do
64 Vine, or *lady's, poire de vigne,* or *de demoiselle*   Nov.
65 Willow leaved, *ornamental*   do
66 Swan's egg, M   November to January.
67 Mansuette   do
68 Newtown virgalieu, M   do
69 Winter thorn, *épine d'hyver,* M   do
70 Winter achan, M   do

82 Louise-bonne, M   do
83 Chaumontelle, *beurré d'hyver, or Bezy de Chaumontelle*, M do
84 Catillac, B   do
85 Easter bergamot, *bergamotte de pásque, or ter-*
    ling, B   December to March.
86 Colmar, *manna, or bergamotte tardivé*   do
87 Ambrette, M   do
88 King's bon chretien, B   do
89 Bon chretien d'Auche, B   January to March.
90 Holland bergamot, *or amoselle*   do
91 Winter rousselette   do
92 Tonneau   do
93 St. Martial, *or poire angelique*, M   do
94 Franc-real, *fine gold of winter, fin or d'hyver*, B   do
95 Silver striped leaved, *ornamental*, 50 cts.   do
96 Uvedale's St. Germain, *or union*, B   do
97 Royal winter, *royale d'hyver*, M   January to April.
98 Winter bon chretien, *bon chretien d'hyver*, B   do
99 Treasure, *tresor d'amour*   January to May.
100 Imperial oak leaved, *Imperiale à feuille de chêne*   do
101 Sarasin   do
102 Taunton squash, P
103 Besberry, P
104 Barland, P   }   *Said to afford Perry equal to*
105 Alduira, P   *Champaign.*
106 Oldfield, P
107 New Holmar, P

Some select kinds are propagated on Quince stocks, for Dwarfs
  or Espaliers.

CHERRIES, 50 Cents. Prunus *Ceras*
Class, *Icosandria*. Order, *Monogynia*.
* denotes fruit of very large size.

1 Early May
2 Early Richmond
3 May duke
4 *Fraser's black tartarian
5 Fraser's white tartarian
6 Black heart
7 White heart
8 Turkey heart
9 American heart
10 Harrison's heart
11 Ronald's black heart, *Ronald's superb, or Circassian*
12 China heart
13 Gascoign's heart
14 Lion's heart
15 *Ox heart
16 *Bleeding heart
17 Amber heart
18 Lundie Gean
19 Transparent Gean
20 Lukeward
21 Graffion, *or Ambrée*
22 *Yellow Spanish
23 Late Spanish
24 Black Spanish, $1
25 Black corone, *or caroon*
26 Holman's, *or June duke*
27 Arch duke
28 *Prince's duke
29 Carnation, *best for preserving*
30 Tradescant's
31 Mazard
32 Honey
33 Hertfordshire white
34 Four-to-the-pound, *or tobacco leaved*, $1
35 Cluster, *cerise à bouquet*, $1
36 Griottier d'Allemagne, $1
37 White transparent Crimea, $1
38 Elton, $1
39 Hertfordshire black, *late black heart*

ripe in

May and

July and

49 Weeping
50 French double blossom, *very large flowers*
51 English double blossom, *smaller flowers*
52 Perfumed, *Prunus mahaleb*
53 All saints, *pendant flowering cluster*

} ornamental do

Some select kinds are propagated for Dwarfs or Espaliers, on Morello stocks, as they are found to succeed well, and produce abundantly.

———

PLUMS, 50 Cents. Prunus *domestica.*
Class, *Icosandria.* Order, *Monogynia.*

† denotes those of large size.
* ——— those of superior flavour.

1 Early Yellow, *jaune hative, or white primordian* ripe in July.
2 *Cherry, *or prune cerizete* do
3 Red chicasaw do
4 Yellow chicasaw do
5 Early damask, *Morocco or damas noir* August.
6 Early coral ⎱ *Native fruits of great beauty, and*
7 Golden drop ⎰ *good bearers.* do
8 Précoce de Tours, *early Tours* do
9 Azure hative, *early azure* do
10 *Early sweet damson, *or damascene* do
11 Chinese double flowering, $ 1 do
12 *Burlington red do
13 French copper do
14 †Blue Holland do
15 *Drap d'or, *cloth of gold, or mirabelle double* do
16 Blue perdrigon September.
17 †German prune, *Guetsche,* $ 1 do

18 Elfreth's prune   *ripe in* September.
19 †Red imperial, *red bonum magnum*   do
20 †Yellow egg, *white bonum magnum, white imperial,*
     or Mogul   do
21 *Large queen Claudia, *grosse reine Claude, or Dau-*
     phine   do
22 Little queen Claudia, *petite reine Claude*   do
23 *†Bolmer's Washington. *This justly celebrated gage*
     plum has weighed near four ounces, $1   do
24 *†Flushing gage, *next in size to the above,* $1   do
25 *Green gage, *gros damas vert*   do
26 *Blue gage   do
27 *Red gage   do
28 *Yellow gage   do
29 *White gage   do
30 †Large red Orleans, *purple egg*   do
31 *†Smith's Orleans   do
32 *White apricot plum, *prune abricottée*   do
33 Fotheringham   do
34 Muscle   do
35 Cheston   do
36 *Red diaper, *roche-carbon, or diaprée rouge*   do
37 Mangeron   do
38 Mirabelle   do
39 Peach plum, *prune pêche,* $1   do
40 Pitless, *prune sans noyeau,* $1   do
41 St Catharine   October.
42 Winesour, *of Yorkshire*   do
43 Monsieur's, *or Wentworth*   do
44 *Imperatrice violette, *Empress, Imperial violet,* or
     prune d'Altesse   do
45 Late cluster   October and November.
46 White damson, *or damascene*   do
47 Winter damson, *or damascene*   November.
48 American dwarf, *or sand cherry, Prunus depressa,*
     ornamental.

A few select kinds are propagated for Dwarfs or Espaliers.

APRICOTS, 37½ Cents. Prunus *Armeniaca*.
Class, *Icosandria*. Order, *Monogynia*.

Those marked thus P are best for preserving.

1 Early masculine, *abricot précoce, or hatif musqué*   July.
2 Large early, *superior*   do
3 Orange, P   do
4 Roman   do
5 Apricot de Nancy, *very superior*   August.
6 Peach, *abricot pêche*, P   do
7 Brussels   do
8 White, *or abricot blanc*   do
9 Gold blotched leaved, *abricot de Messine*   do
10 Algiers, *abricot d'Angers, with sweet pits*   do
11 Portugal   do
12 Breda   do
13 Moorpark, *or Anson's*   do
14 Turkey   do
16 Black, *or Pope's, noir du Pape, or abricot violet*   do
16 Alberge, *with sweet pits*, P   do

Some select kinds are propagated for Dwarfs or Espaliers.

———

PEACHES, 37½ Cents. Amygdalus *Persica*.
Class, *Icosandria*. Order, *Monogynia*.

[The varieties of Peaches are so extensive, that the number might easily be increased to two hundred; but, as it is generally preferred to have a moderate number of the best kinds to ripen in succession, the following have been selected on account of their size, flavour, or time of ripening, from among the best kinds imported from Europe, as well as from such as have originated in America.]

    * denotes those of superior flavour.
    † ——— those of remarkable size.
    M ——— those which are melting.
    C ——— Clingstones or Pavies.

1 Scarlet nutmeg, *avant rouge, or pêche de Troyes*   July.
2 *Yellow nutmeg, *avant jaune*   do
3 Red nutmeg   do
4 *White nutmeg, *avant blanche*   do
5 *Green nutmeg, *early Anne*   do
6 *Sweet water, *or large American nutmeg*, M   August.

7 *Red rareripe, M	*ripe in* August.
8 *White rareripe, *free stone heath*	do
9 Yellow rareripe, M	do
10 White magdalen, *madeleine blanche*	do
11 Early red, C	do
12 Early white, C	do
13 Portugal, C	do
14 Belle chevreuse, M	do
15 Early Newington, C	do
16 *†Large early, *York rareripe*, M	do
17 Heath	do
18 Golden purple, C	do
19 *Grosse mignonne, *veloutée de Merlet*, M	September.
20 Petite mignonne, *double de Troyes*	do
21 *Millet's mignonne	do
22 Early purple, *pourprée hative*, M	do
23 Royal George, *la royale*, M	do
24 Royal Charlotte, M	do
25 *Royal Kensington, M	do
26 *†Old mixon	do
27 *Old Newington, C	do
28 *Bourdine, *or narbonne*, M	do
29 Nivette, *nivette veloutée*, M	do
30 Montauban, M	do
31 *†Malta, M	do
32 Noblesse, M	do
33 Cut leaved	do
34 *†Columbia	do
35 Washington, C	do
36 *†Pine apple, C	do
37 *†Kennedy's Carolina, *early lemon*, C	do
38 *†Green Catharine, M	do
39 *†Red cheek malacoton, M	do
40 White malacoton	do
41 Bellegarde, *or Galande*, M	do
42 *Orange peach, M	do
43 Orange, C	do
44 †President	do
45 †Congress, C	do
46 *Late purple, *pourprée tardive, smooth skin like a nectarine*, M	do
47 *†Late admirable, *Bellis, or belle de Vitry*, C	do
48 White blossom	do
49 *Double blossom, *or rose peach, very ornamental*, 50 *cts.* do

68 †Barcelona yellow, C   do
69 *†Pompone, *pavie rouge de pompone*, C M   do
70 *†Heath. *This tree should be kept in cultivated ground, and the fruit ripened in the house; it is by many thought superior to all other peaches*, C   October & November.
71 Gough's late red, C   do
72 White winter, *white at the stone*, C   do
73 Green winter, C   November and December.
74 Algiers yellow winter, C   do

Some select kinds are inoculated low, suitable for Dwarfs or Espaliers.

———

NECTARINES, 37½ Cents. Amygdalus *Persica var. fructo glabro.* Class, *Icosandria.* Order, *Monogynia.*

C denotes Clingstones.

1 Early scarlet   *ripe in* August.
2 Fairchild's early, C   do
3 Elruge   September.
4 Argyle   do
5 Golden, *jaune lisse*, C   do
6 Newington, C   do
7 Aromatic   do

C

8 Temple's   *ripe in* September.
9 Red Roman, C   do
10 Vermash   do
11 Peterborough   do
12 Green, C   October.
13 White, C

———

1 Hard shell, *or bitter*   October.
2 Thin shell,   *andier des dames*   do
3   *Sultane*   do
4 Large Jordan, *gros cassante*

———

            October.
2 Pear   do
3 Portugal, *or eatable*   November to March.
4 Winter

———

1 Large Black European, } Morus nigra
  50 *cts.*
2 Red American   ——— rubra
3 White Chinese, *or Ita-* } ——— alba
  lian, for silk-worms
4 Japan paper, *ornamental*   Broussonetia papyrifera

FIGS, 50 Cents. Ficus *Carica*.
Class, *Polygamia*. Order, *Triæcia*.

1 Early brown, *the best bearer*
2 Large late brown
3 Large white Genoa
4 Ischia
5 Marseilles yellow
6 Brown Malta
7 Large blue

———

CURRANTS, 25 Cents.
Class, *Pentandria*. Order, *Monogynia*.

1 Large Dutch red Ribes rubrum
2 Large Dutch white —— *v. fructo albo*
3 Champagne, *pale red transparent* } —— *v. fructo roseo*
4 Striped leaved, *beautiful, 50 cts.* } —— *v. fol. variegato*
5 Black English —— nigrum
6 Black American —— floridum
7 Hawthorn leaved, $1 —— oxycanthoides
8 Lewis's fragrant currant, *with yellow flowers of a delightful odour, and black fruit, 50 cts.* } —— aureum
9 Do. *with yellow fruit and scentless flowers, 50 cts.* } —— *v. inodora*
10 Indian currant, *with red fruit in autumn and winter, 37 cts.* } Symphoria glomerata
11 Snowberry, *with clusters of beautiful white fruit in autumn, extremely ornamental, 50 cts.* } —— racemosa

RASPBERRIES. Rubus *idæus*.
Class, *Icosandria*. Order, *Polygynia*.

1 English red, *best for brandy, and the kind usually cul-*
  tivated for market, 10 cts.   *ripe in* June & July.
2 English white, 12½ cts.   do
3 Brentford red, 12½ cts.   do
4 Brentford white, 25 cts.   do
5 Antwerp red, 25 cts.   July and August.
6 Antwerp white, or yellow, 25 cts.   do
7 Large fruited cane, 12½ cts.   July and October.
8 Beehive, 25 ts.   do
9 Ford's prolific, 25 cts.   do
10 Twice bearing, 12½ cts.   do
11 Barnet red, 25 cts.   July.
12 American black, *Rubus occidentalis*, 10 cts. do
13 American white, —— —————— *v. albo*, 12½ cts. do
14 American red, *Rubus strigosus*, 12½ cts.   do
15 Canada purple rose flowering, *ornamental*, 25 cts. August.

*GOOSEBERRIES, Ribes *Uva-crispa*.
Class, *Pentandria*.   Order, *Monogynia*.
Different kinds by name, 31¼ Cents.
Do. do. mixed, 25 Cents.

[Of this fruit near 400 varieties have been imported from England, where they excel in its cultivation, especially in Lancashire and Yorkshire; and where they frequently weigh from one to one and a half ounces. The following have been selected on account of their large size, flavour, or time of ripening, and many of them have, in turns, obtained the premiums at the annual exhibitions in England.]

Red.

1 Alcock's king	11 Fisher's conqueror
2 ——— duke of York	12 Lomax's victory
3 Brundrit's Atlas	13 Milling's crown bob
4 Warrington	14 Leigh's rifleman
5 Ironmonger	15 Bratherton's pasttime
6 Shaw's Billy Dean	16 Hargraw's major Hill
7 Bullfinch	17 Turner's Lincoln
8 Large amber	18 Walker's Bank of Eng-
9 Smooth claret	land
10 Dean's glory of England	19 Rumbullion

White.

20 Elephant
21 Snowball
22 Highland
23 White heart
24 Callebank's
25 Crystal
26 Leigh's fiddler

27 Grundy's fowler
28 ———— milk maid
29 Saunder's royal oak
30 Samson's queen Anne
31 Holding's white muslin
32 Hilton's blunderbuss

Yellow.

33 Golden drop
34 Rocket's
35 Long yellow
36 Rough yellow
37 Golden seedling
38 Golden taper

39 Prince of Orange
40 Hutton's goldfinch
41 Royal yellow
42 Taylor's golden talent
43 Hill's royal sovereign
44 Gradwell's ville de Paris

Green.

45 Early hairy
46 Gascoign
47 Walnut
48 Satisfaction
49 Dorrington
50 Ne plus ultra

51 Green oak
52 Duke of Bedford
53 Ribbed
54 Blakeley's chisel
55 Allen's glory of Ratcliffe

STRAWBERRIES, 25 Cents per Dozen.
Fragaria *vesca.* Class, *Polyandria.* Order, *Monogynia.*

1 Morrissania, *or early scarlet Virginian*   *ripe in* May.
2 English red wood   June.
3 English white wood, *white hautboy*   do
4 English red hautboy   do
5 Large Hudson   } *These are the kinds cultivated*
6 Red Chili, 37 *cts.*   }   *for market*   June and July.
7 Blush, *or green Chili, fraisier-vert,* 37 *cts.*   do
8 Bourbon blush, 50 *cts.*   do
9 Pine apple, *fraisier-ananas,* 50 *cts.*   do
10 Caroline, 50 *cts.*   do
11 Black, $ 1   do
12 Red alpine, *monthly, or everbearing. It is pre-*
    ferable to make a new bed of this kind every year,
    50 *cts.*   June to December.
13 White alpine, 50 *cts.*   do

ASPARAGUS.

Roots *per hundred,* $ 1
Ditto *per thousand,* $ 8

———

GRAPES.   Vitis *vinifera.*
Class, *Pentandria.*   Order, *Monogynia.*

37½ Cents, except those noted.

[The foreign Grapes included in the following assortment are reared from plants imported *directly* from the first collections in France, and descriptions of nearly all of them will be found in the most celebrated works on the culture of the Vine—such as Speechley, Duhammel, Forsyth, &c.— and also in the Treatise attached to this Catalogue. Many of them will be found to differ essentially from fruits cultivated under similar names in some parts of the United States; as in many instances the possessors of Grapes of doubtful origin have attached to them the names of old established fruits. This practice, so common in our country, and so calculated to disseminate error, cannot be too greatly deprecated.]

C denotes those which ripen well in the City only.

C C ———— which ripen well both in City and Country.

C C F ———— which succeed in the Country in fine seasons.

1 Earliest French, *Vigne précoce,* C C   ripe in August.
2 Early white muscadine, *or summer sweet water,* C C   do
3 July grape, *morillon noir hatif,* or early black cluster. C C   do
4 Large black cluster, C C   September.
5 Small black cluster, *or Burgundy,* C C   do
6 Miller's Burgundy, *or Meunier,* C C   do
7 Auvergne noir, *true Burgundy, or black morillon,* C C   do
8 White sweet water, C C F   do
9 Black   do   C C   do
10 Black Madeira, C C   do
11 Purple   do   C C   do
12 Bordeaux purple, C C   do
13 White Frontignac, *muscat blanc,* C C, $ 1   do
14 Grizzly   do.   C C, 50 *cts.*   do
15 Black, *or purple* do. *muscat noir, or black Constantia,* C C, 50 *cts.*   do
16 Red do. *muscat rouge,* C C F, 50 *cts.*   October.

17 Blue, or violet do. *muscat violet*, C C, $ 1 *ripe in* October.
18 White muscat of Alexandria, *or Alexandrian Frontignac, muscat blanc d'Alexandrie*, C, $ 1   do
19 White Chasselas, *Royal Muscadine, D'Arboyce, or
Chasselas blanc*, C C, 50 cts.   do
20 Red Chasselas, *chasselas rouge*, C C F, 50 cts.   do
21 Rose do. *chasselas rose*, C C, $ 1   do
22 Musk do. *chasselas musquée, or Frankindale*. C C, $ 1   do
23 Cut leaved do. *chasselas à feuilles lasciniés*, $ 1   do
24 Black Hamburgh, C C   do
25 Red do or *Gibraltar*, C C, 50 cts.   do
26 Parsley leaved, *or Ciotat*, C C F, 50 cts.   do
27 Chocolate coloured, C C   do
28 Red muscadel, *muscadelle rouge*, C, 50 cts.   do
29 White Constantia, C, $ 1   do
30 White, *or true Tokay*, C C F, $ 1   do
31 Lombardy, *flame coloured Tokay, or Rhenish*, C C F, $ 1 do
32 Malvoisie, *Malmsey, or blue Tokay*, C C, $ 1   do
33 St. Peter's, *black*, C C F, 50 cts.   do
34 Bland's pale red, C C   do
35 White Cornishon, *cornishon blanc*, C, $ 1   do
36 Syrian, *with monstrous bunches, white*, C, $ 1   do
37 Black, *or seedless Corinth, or currant, Corinthé
sans pepins.* $ 1   do
38 Small blue Corinth, *Corinthe violet*, $ 1   do
39 Luscious white, *blanc doux*, $ 1
40 Sauvignon's white, 50 cts.
41 White Calabrian, *blanc de la Calabre*, $ 1
42 Violet do. *violet de la Calabre*, $ 1
43 Striped grape, *culotte de Suisse*, $ 1
44 La rousse de Lyons, $ 1

AMERICAN NATIVE GRAPES.

45 Early white   *ripe in* August.
46 Isabella, *from South-Carolina*   September.
47 Scuppernon, *from North-Carolina*   do
48 Alexander's, Skuylkill muscadel, *or Spring Mill
Constantia*   do
49 Orwigsburg, *white*   do
50 Elsingburg, *blue*   do
51 Catawba Tokay, *purple*   do

52 Carolina muscadine   *ripe in* September.
53 Worthington, *black, found near Annapolis*   do
54 Elkton
55 Norton's Virginia seedling
56 Prince Edward, *from Virginia*
57 Purple fox

The following French Grapes are under cultivation, but will not be for sale until the autumn of 1824, $1 each.

58 White morillon, *morillon blanc,* C C F
59 Variegated do.   *morillon panaché*
60 Malmsey muscadine, *Malvoisie musquée, white,* C C F
61 White muscat of Lunel, *muscat blanc de Lunel,* C C F
62 Red muscat of Alexandria, *muscat rouge d'Alexandrie,* C
63 Red muscat of Jerusalem, C
64 White Burgundy, *Penu blanc*
65 Black Lisbon, C C F
66 Black muscadel, *muscadelle noir,* C
67 Variegated Chasselas, *chasselas panaché*
68 Small black   do.   *chasselas noir petit*
69 Chasselas de Fontenoy
70 Black muscadine, *muscadine noir,* C C F
71 Black raisin, C
72 Red   do.
73 White   do. C
74 Red Constantia
75 White Hamburgh, *or Portugal,* C
76 White Corinth, *Corinthe blanc,* C C F
77 Le cœur, *or Morocco, grizzly,* C
78 Black Damascus, C
79 Brick, *pale red,* C C
80 Claret, *black,* C C F
81 Black Prince, C
82 Smyrna, *red,* C C F
83 Black Spanish, *or Alicant, Grosnoir d'Espagne,* C C F
84 Aleppo, *white. black, and striped on same bunch,* C C F
85 Golden Galician, *yellow,* C
86 Mottled leaved grape, *vigne à feuilles panachés*
87 Verjus, *or verjuice*
88 Calliaba
89 Verdots
90 Trois Keiottes

ORNAMENTAL FOREST TREES of the first class and largest growth, esteemed for their foliage, flowers, or fruit. 37½ Cents, except those noted.

1 White flowering horse chesnut, 50 *to* 75 *cts.* — Aesculus hippocastanum

2 Yellow flowering do. 50 *cts.* ——— flava

3 Sugar maple, 50 *cts.* — Acer saccharinum

4 Scarlet do. *with clusters of showy flowers in March* — ——— rubrum

5 Norway maple, 50 *cts.* ——— platanoides

6 English do. 50 *cts.* ——— campestre

7 European sycamore, 50 *cts.* ——— pseudoplatanus

8 Chinese ailanthus, *or tree of heaven,* * *with leaves four feet long,* $1 — Ailanthus glandulosa

9 European autumn flowering alder, 50 *cts.* — Alnus glutinosa

10 European cut leaved do. 50 *cts.* — ——— *v. lasciniata*

11 Scotch weeping birch, *of poetic celebrity,* 50 *cts.* — Betula alba-*pendula*

12 Yellow birch ——— excelsa

13 Canada canoe birch ——— papyracea

14 Black birch, 25 *cts.* ——— lenta

15 Paper birch, 25 *cts.* ——— populifolia

16 Spanish chesnut, *with large eatable fruit,* 50 *cts.* — Castanea vesca

17 American do. 25 *cts.* ——— americana

18 Catalpa, *much admired for its showy flowers,* 50 *cts.* — Catalpa syringæfolia

19 American cypress, *of fine appearance and very quick growth,* 50 *cts.* — Cupressus disticha

20 European ash, *very stately. and of rapid growth,* 50 *cts.* — Fraxinus excelsior

* This tree is so called in Japan on account of the enormous height to which it attains. It has the quality of withstanding the greatest heat uninjured, and retains its foliage until very late in the season.

21 Honey locust, *or thorny acacia* } Gleditschia triacanthos

22 Kentucky coffee, *or bon-duc, of singular growth, with spikes of purple flowers,* 50 cts. } Gymnocladus canadensis

23 Madeira nut, *or English walnut,* 50 cts. } Juglans regia

24 French double-do. $ 1 ———— *v. major*

25 Round black walnut ———— nigra

26 Butternut ———— cinerea

27 Pecan, *or Illinois nut,* 50 cts. ———— olivæformis

28 Hiccory nuts, *eight species, each* 25 cts. }

29 Sassafras, 25 cts. Laurus sassafras

30 Maple leaved sweet gum Liquidamber styraciflua

31 Tulip tree, *or white wood, very stately and ornamental,* 50 cts. } Liriodendron tulipifera

32 Pride of India, *with clusters of purple flowers, and very beautiful foliage,* 50 cts. } Melia azedarach

33 European larch, *or deciduous fir,* 50 cts. } Pinus larix

34 American do. *or hackmatack,* 50 cts. } ——— pendula

35 American plane, *sycamore, or buttonwood,* 25 cts. } Platanus occidentalis

36 Oriental plane, 50 cts. ———— orientalis

37 Striped do. $ 1 ———— *fol. variegate*

38 Lombardy poplar Populus dilatata

39 White leaved do. *or abele, very ornamental,* 50 cts. } ——— alba

40 Athenian do. ——— græca

41 Balsam do. *or tacmahac* ——— balsamifera

42 Carolina do. *or cotton tree* ——— angulata

43 Canada do. ——— monilifera

44 Water do. ——— heterophylla

45 American aspen do. ——— trepida

46 European aspen do. ——— tremula

47 American bird cherry, 50 *cts.* Prunus virginiana

48 European bird cherry, 50 *cts.* Prunus padus

49 English royal oak, *celebrated for being the refuge of King Charles II.* 50 cts.   Quercus robur

50 Lucombe's oak, $1   ——— *v. exoniensis*

51 Turkey oak, 50 *cts.*   ——— cerris

52 Fox's white oak. *These are raised from seeds of the two trees under which George Fox, the original Quaker, preached; which trees are still in a thriving state at Flushing*   ——— alba

53 Willow leaved oak, 50 *cts.*   ——— phellos

54 American oaks, *twenty-two species, each* 25 *cts.*

55 Common locust, *a superior timber tree,* 25 *cts.*   Robinia pseudacacia

56 ——— *seedlings, two feet high,* $3 *per* 100

57 ——— *do. four do.* $5 *per* 100

58 Weeping willow, 37 *to* 50*cts.*   Salix babylonica

59 Upright green willow   ——— alba

60 Golden willow   ——— vitellina

61 European linden, *or lime, much admired, and very ornamental,* 50 *cts.*   Tilia europæa

62 Red twigged do, 50 *cts.*   ——— parviflora

63 American do. *or* bass-wood, 50 *cts.*   ——— americana

64 Scotch, *or witch elm,* 50 *cts.*   Ulmus montana

65 English elm, 50 *cts.*   ——— campestris

66 Curled leaved do. 75 *cts.*   ——— *var. crispa*

67 Dutch, *or cork barked do.* 50 *cts.*   ——— suberosa

68 Weeping do. 50 *cts.*   ——— pendula

69 Wahoo do. 50 *cts.*   ——— alata

ORNAMENTAL FOREST TREES of the second class, and middle-growth, esteemed for their foliage and flowers. 37½ Cents, except those noted.

1 Sensitive tree, *with beautiful foliage*, 50 cts.	Acacia julibrissin
2 Silver striped sycamore, *very ornamental*, $ 1	Acer pseudoplatanus, *fol. arg. varieg.*
3 Scarlet flowering horse chesnut, 50 cts.	Aesculus pavia
4 Papaw, *or custard apple*, 50 cts.	Anona glabra
5 Prickly ash, *angelica, or Herculus's club*	Aralia spinosa
6 European Judas tree, *with very showy flowers, which appear before the leaves,* 50 cts.	Cercis siliquastrum
7 American do. *with flowers as above*, 50 cts.	——— canadensis
8 Snowdrop, *or white fringe tree, with flowers resembling cut paper,* 50 cts.	Chionanthus virginica
9 White flowering dogwood, 25 cts.	Cornus florida
10 White leaf, *or white beam*, 50 cts.	Cratægus aria
11 Azarole, 50 cts.	——— azarolus
12 Laburnum, *much admired for its clusters of bright yellow flowers,* 50 cts.	Cytisus laburnum
13 Scotch do. 50 cts.	——— alpinus
14 Persimmon, *or American medlar*, 50 cts.	Diospyros virginica
15 European beech	Fagus sylvatica
16 Purple, *or copper leaved beech,* $ 1	——— v. purpurea
17 Weeping ash, *of singular appearance*, 50 cts.	Fraxinus excelsior, *v. pendula*
18 Curled leaved ash, *of very curious growth*, 50 cts.	——— atra

19 Flowering ash, 50 *cts.* — Fraxinus ornus
20 Chinese do. $ 1 — ———— chinensis
21 Chinese thorny acacia, $ 1 — Gleditschia sinensis
22 Umbrella magnolia, *with very large white fragrant flowers, 50 cts.* — Magnolia tripetela
23 Glaucous magnolia, *with flowers of exquisite fragrance, 50 cts.* — ———— glauca
24 Double flowering do. $ 3 — ———— *v. pleno*
25 Splendid magnolia, *with leaves two to three feet long, and flowers twelve inches in diameter, of a delightful fragrance,* $ 2 — ———— macrophylla
26 Great flowering evergreen magnolia, $ 1 — ———— grandiflora
27 Blue flowering magnolia, *or cucumber tree,* 50 *cts.* — ———— acuminata
28 Ear-leaved magnolia, $ 2 — ———— auriculata
29 Yellow flowering magnolia. $ 3 — ———— cordata
30 German, *or Dutch medlar,* 50 *cts.* — Mespilus germanica
31 Snowy medlar, *so called from its being covered with white flowers early in spring* — Pyrus botryapium
32 Chinese double rose flowering apple, 50 *cts.* — ———— spectabilis
33 Japan scarlet flowering do. $ 1 — ———— japonica
34 Woolly, *or sage leaved pear,* 50 *cts.* — ———— pollveria
35 Willow leaved do. 50 *cts.* — ———— salicifolia
36 Mount Sinai do. $ 1 — ———— Sinai
37 Venetian sumach, *or purple fringe tree. This beautiful tree is covered during summer with tufts of russet-coloured down, and forms the most singular ornament of the garden,* 50 *cts.* — Rhus cotinus

D

38 European tanners' su-mach, 50 cts. — Rhus coriaria

39 Purple acacia, *with clus-ters of beautiful flowers* — Robinia viscosa

40 Black willow, *of singular appearance* — Salix nigra

41 English common osier —— viminalis

*42 English basket osier —— fissa

43 European mountain ash, or *ScotchRoan, very much admired both for the beau-ty of its foliage and its clusters of scarlet fruit, which remain on many months,* 50 cts. — Sorbus aucuparia

44 American mountain ash, 50 cts. —— americana

45 Bastard mountain ash, 50cts. —— hybrida

46 European sorb, *or service-tree,* 50 cts. —— domestica

47 Tooth-ache tree, *or thorny ash* — Zanthoxylum fraxineum

———

ORNAMENTAL SHRUBS, esteemed for their flowers, foliage, or fruit. 25 Cents, except those noted.

1 Dwarf white flowering horse chesnut, 50 cts. — Aesculus macrostachya

Indigo shrub, *with spikes of blue flowers,* 37 cts. — Amorpha fruticosa

3 Double flowering almond, *beautiful,* 50 cts. — Amygdalus pumila, *pleno*

4 Andromeda, *many species* — Andromeda, *sp.*

5 Southern wood — Artemesia abrotanum

6 Groundsel tree, *covered in autumn with white fea-thered tufts, very orna-mental,* 50 cts. — Baccharis halimifolia

7 Barberry, *for preserves* — Berberis canadensis

8 Purple flowering Calycan-
thus, *or sweet' scented* Calycanthus floridus
shrub, 50 *cts.*

9 Brown flowering do. 50 *cts.* —————— glaucus

10 Chinquapin, *or dwarf gar-* Castanea pumila
den chesnut, 50 *cts.*

11 Prince's ditto, *with large* —————— *v. Princei*
fruit, 50 *cts.*

12 Clethra, *with very fra-* Clethra alnifolia
grant flowers in autumn

13 Yellow flowering Bladder-
senna, *blooming both in* Colutea arborescens
spring and autumn, 37 *cts.*

14 Red flowering do. 50 *cts.* —————— cruenta

15 Pocock's do. 50 *cts.* —————— Pocockii

16 Scorpion senna, *or red* Coronilla emerus
Coronilla, 37 *cts.*

17 Sweet fern, *leaves very* Comptonia asplenifolia
fragrant

18 Double yellow Japan globe
flower, *blooming both in* Corchorus japonicus
spring and autumn, $1

19 Myrtle leaved Coriaria, $1 Coriaria myrtifolia

20 Bloody dogwood, *in au-*
tumn and winter the
branches are of a beauti- Cornus sanguinea
ful crimson, 37 *cts.*

21 Blue berried do. 37 *cts.* —————— sericea

22 Cornelian cherry, *with long*
scarlet fruit in autumn, —————— mascula
very ornamental, 50 *cts.*

23 English white filbert, 37 *cts.* Corylus avellana-*alba*

24 do. red do. 25 *cts* —————— *v. rubra*

25 Large Spanish do. *Barce-* —————— *v. major*
lona, or cob-nut, 37 *cts.*

26 American hazelnut —————— americana

27 European common hawthorn Cratægus oxycantha

28 Double white flowering
hawthorn, *with beautiful*
flowers resembling small —————— *v. pleno*
roses, which change to
purple, 50 *cts.*

29 Scarlet flowering haw- —————— *v. roseo*
thorn, 50 *cts.*

30 Cluster flowered Cytisus, 50 cts. — Cytisus capitatus

31 Sessile leaved do. 50 cts. — ——— sessilifolius

32 Pink mezereon, *blooming in March, with flowers of delightful fragrance* — Daphne mezereum.

33 White flowering do. 50 cts. — ——— *v. album*

34 Trailing daphne, $1 — ——— cneorum

35 American strawberry tree, *or burning bush* — Euonymus americanus

36 European broad leaved do. 50 cts. — ——— europæus

37 White fruited do. 50 cts. — ——— *v. fructo albo*

38 Warted do. 50 cts. — ——— verrucosus

39 Franklinia, *with flowers of delightful fragrance,* $1 — Gordonia pubescens

40 Snowdrop, *or silver bell, with wreaths of beautiful flowers in April,* 50 cts. — Halesia tetraptera

41 Witch hazel, *blooming in autumn,* 50 cts. — Hamamelis virginica

42 Single white althæa frutex — Hibiscus syriacus

43 Single red do. — ——— *v. rubro*

44 Double purple do. 37 cts. — ——— *v. purp. pl.*

45 Double white do. 37 cts. — ——— *v. albo pl.*

46 Double pheasant-eyed do. 50 cts. — ——— *v. bicolor*

47 Variegated leaved do. 50 cts. — ——— *v. fol. varieg.*

48 Changeable Hydrangea, *blue and rose-coloured, very showy and ornamental,* 50 cts. — Hydrangea hortensis

49 White flowering do. — ——— vulgaris

50 Oak leaved do. 50 cts. — ——— quercifolia

51 St. John's wort, *with showy flowers,* 37 cts. — Hypericum kalmianum

52 Fœtid do. 37 cts. — ——— hircinum

53 Virginian Itea, 50 cts. — Itea virginica

54 European small leaved yellow jasmine, 37 cts. — Jasminum humile

55 Italian large leaved yellow do. 37 cts. — ——— fruticans

56 Spice wood, *or wild alspice* — Laurus benzoin

57 Willow leaved do. 50 cts. — ——— æstivalis

57 Common privet, *or prim* — Ligustrum vulgare
58 Yellow berried do. 37 *cts.* — ——— *v. fructo flava*
59 Striped leaved do. 37 *cts.* — ——— *v. fol. variegato*
60 Candleberry myrtle, *the berries are used in making candles, and impart an agreeable fragrance* — Myrica cerifera
61 Sweet gale, 37 *cts.* — ——— gale
62 Cranberry — Oxycoccus macrocarpus
63 Carolina large flowering syringo, 37 *cts.* — Philadelphus inodorus
64 European fragrant do. — ——— coronarius
65 Double flowering do. 50 *cts.* — ——— *v. pleno*
66 Striped leaved do. *beautiful,* 75 *cts.* — ——— *v. varieg.*
67 Shrubby cinquefoil, 37 *cts.* — Potentilla fruticosa
68 Winterberry, *covered in autumn and winter with bright scarlet berries* — Prinos verticillatus
69 Dwarf cluster flowering plum, 50 *cts.* — Prunus depressa
70 White blossom sloe, *or English black thorn,* 50 *cts.* — ——— spinosa
71 Trefoil tree, 37 *cts.* — Ptelia trifoliata
72 Christ's thorn, *of the Holy Land,* 50 *cts.* — Rhamnus paliurus
73 Purging sea buckthorn, 37 *cts.* — ——— catharticus
74 Lewis's fragrant yellow flowering currant, *with flowers of a delightful odour, two kinds,* 50 *cts.* — Ribes aureum
75 Rose acacia, *much admired,* 37 *cts.* — Robinia hispida
76 Salt tree robinia, $2 — ——— halacodendron
77 Japan maiden hair, *or jingo tree,* $2 — Salisburia adiantifolia
78 Sweet flowering willow, 37 *cts.* — Salix lucida
79 English variegated willow, *with leaves beautifully mottled,* 37 *cts.* — ——— caprea, *varieg.*
80 Parsley leaved elder, 37 *cts.* — Sambucus nigra *apiifol.*
81 Striped bittersweet, 75 *cts.* — Solanum dulcamara, *v.*

82 Scotch broom, 37 *cts.*	Spartium scoparium
83 Nine-bark spiræa, 37 *cts.*	Spiræa opulifolia
84 Red spiræa	———— tomentosa
85 White do.	———— salicifolia
86 Siberian do. 50 *cts.*	———— lævigata
87 Hypericum leaved ditto, *beautiful,* 37 *cts.*	———— hypericifolia
88 Three leaved bladder-nut, *producing seeds in bladders,* 37 *cts.*	Staphylea trifoliata
89 Five leaved do. 50 *cts.*	———— pinnata
90 Stewartia, $ 1	Stewartia marylandica
91 Snowberry, *with clusters of snow white fruit in autumn, very ornamental,* 50 *cts.*	Symphoria racemosa
92 Indian currant, *with red fruit in autumn and winter,* 37 *cts.*	———— glomerata
93 White lilac, 37 *cts.*	Syringa vulgaris
94 Purple do.	———— *v. purp.*
95 Purple Persian lilac, 50 *cts.*	———— persica
96 White Persian do. $ 1	———— *v. albo*
97 Chinese cut leaved do. *very delicate,* 50 *cts.*	———— *v. lasciniata*
98 Siberian lilac, $ 1	———— sibirica
99 French tamarisk, *much admired*	Tamarix gallica
100 Huckleberry, *many species*	Vaccinium, *sp.*
101 Snowball, *or guelder rose,* 37 *cts.*	Viburnum opulus
102 Cranberry viburnum, *with clusters of fruit resembling cranberries*	———— oxycoccus
103 Wayfaring tree, 50 *cts.*	———— lantana
104 Rose leaved viburnum	———— pubescens
105 Chaste tree, *very fragrant,* 37 *cts.*	Vitus agnus-castus
106 Parsley leaved Zanthorhiza	Zanthorhiza apiifolia

ORNAMENTAL EVERGREENS, 50 Cents,
except those noted.

Those marked thus * require a slight protection in winter—there are many other Evergreens which will stand the winters of the Southern States, and which will be found under the Green-House head.

1 Common box, 12 cts.   Buxus sempervirens
2 Silver striped do. 25 cts.   ——— v. arg. varieg.
3 Gold striped do.   ——— v. aur. varieg.
4 White cedar   Cupressus thyoides
5 *European cypress, $1   ——— sempervirens
6 Shrubby horse tail, of very curious growth   Ephedra distachya
7 American holly   Ilex opaca
8 European holly   ——— aquifolium
9 *Silver striped do. $1   ——— v. arg. variegato
10 *Gold striped do. $1   ——— v. aur. variegato
11 *Gold blotched do. $1   ——— v. aur. maculato
12 *Box leaved do. $1   ——— v. buxifolia
13 *Hedgehog do. $1   ——— v. echinatum
14 *Gold striped hedgehog do. $1   ——— ——— aur.
15 *Silver striped do. $1   ——— ——— arg.
16 Swedish upright juniper   Juniperus suecia
17 Red American cedar, 25 cts.   ———virginica
18 European savin, celebrated for its cures of horses   ——— sabina
19 Variegated savin   ——— v. varieg.
20 Broad leaved kalmia, or laurel, 37 cts.   Kalmia latifolia
21 Narrow leaved do. very delicate, 37 cts.   ——— angustifolia
22 *European sweet-bay, $1   Laurus nobilis
23 Italian evergreen privet, 25 cts.   Ligustrum vulgare, v.
24 Evergreen thorn, with scarlet fruit during autumn and winter, very ornamental, 37 cts.   Mespilus pyracantha
25 Balm of Gilead, or balsam fir, very much admired,   Pinus balsamea
    4 feet high, 50 cts.
    5 to 6 feet high, 75 cts.
    8 feet, $1 50 cts.

26 White, *or Weymouth pine,*
   much admired, 50 cts.   Pinus strobus
   75 cts. $1, *and* $1 50,
   as in size

27 Norway spruce fir   —— abies
28 Red spruce fir   —— rubra
29 Black, *or double spruce fir* —— nigra
30 White spruce fir   —— alba
31 Hemlock, *or drooping* —— canadensis
   spruce fir
32 Cedar of Lebanon, $2   —— cedrus
33 European silver fir   —— picea
34 Scotch mountain fir   —— sylvestris
35 Pinaster, *or cluster pine,* $1 —— pinaster
36 Italian stone pine, *with* —— pinea
   eatable fruit, $1
37 Siberian stone pine, $2 —— cembra
38 Pitch, *or resin pine*   —— rigida
39 Yellow pine   —— variabilis
40 *Carolina plum, *or wild* Prunus caroliniensis
   orange,* $1
41 *English laurel, $1   —— laurocerasus
42 *Portugal laurel, $1   —— lusitanica
43 *Spanish cork tree, $1   Quercus suber
44 *English evergreen oak —— ilex
45 *American live oak   —— virens
46 Purple pontic Rhododen- Rhododendron ponticum
   dron, *beautiful,* $1
47 Double do. $2   —— *v. pleno*
48 American do.   —— maximum
49 *Alexandrian, *or poetic
   laurel, of classic cele-* Ruscus racemosus
   brity, $1
50 Prickly leaved butcher's —— aculeatus
   broom, $1
51 *Double leaved do. $1 —— hypoglossum
52 English yew, *the principal
   ornament of the church-* Taxus baccata
   yards in England
53 American do.   —— canadensis
54 Chinese arbor vitæ, *very* Thuya orientalis
   ornamental
55 American do.   —— occidentalis

VINES and CREEPERS, for covering walls or arbours, 25 Cents, except where noted.

1 American ivy	Ampelopsis quinquefolia
2 Heart leaved do. *37 cts.*	————— cordifolia
3 Pipe vine, *or birthwort, with very large leaves, and flowers like a Dutch pipe,* 50 *cts.*	Aristolochia sipho
4 American atragene, $1	Atragene americana
5 Austrian do. $1	————— alpina
6 Siberian do. $1	————— siberica
7 Scarlet trumpet creeper, 50 *cts.*	Bignonia radicans
8 Chinese great flowering do. $1	————— grandiflora
9 Cross bearing bignonia, 50*cts.*	————— crucigera
10 American bittersweet	Celastrus scandens
11 White flowering virgin's bower	Clematis virginica
12 Curled flowered do. 37 *cts.*	————— crispa
13 Red flowering do. 50 *cts.*	————— viticella
14 Blue flowering do. 50 *cts.*	————— *v. cœrulea*
15 Double blue do. $1	————— *v. pleno*
16 Leather flowered do. 37 *cts.*	————— viorna
17 Traveller's joy, 50 *cts.*	————— vitalba
18 Carolina yellow jasmine, 50 *cts.*	Gelseminum nitidum
19 Cluster flowering glycine, *beautiful,* 37 *cts.*	Glycine frutescens
20 Evergreen ivy, 37 *cts.*	Hedera helix
21 Yellow berried ivy, 50 *cts.*	————— *v. fructo flava*
22 Striped leaved do. 50 *cts.*	————— *v. variegato*
23 White flowering jasmine, 37 *cts.*	Jasminum officinale
24 Gold striped do. $1	————— *v. aur. varieg.*
25 Silver striped do. $1	————— *v. arg. varieg.*
26 Honeysuckles. *See page* 46	Lonicera, *sp.*
27 Box thorn, *or matrimony vine, producing its flowers in pairs*	Lycium europæum
28 Canadian moonseed	Menispermum canadense

29 Periploca, *or Virginian silk; with very curious flowers,* 37 cts. — Periploca græca

30 Multiflora rose, 50 cts. — Rosa multiflora

31 Scotch creeping do. 50 cts. —— procera

32 Sweetbriar, *many kinds. See page* 48 —— rubiginosa

33 Double rose flowering bramble, 50 cts. — Rubus fruticosus, *plene*

34 White fruited do. 50 cts. —— v. albo

35 English nightshade, *or bittersweet* — Solanum dulcamara

36 Periwinkle, *or evergreen myrtle* — Vinca minor

37 Gold striped do. *with white and blue flowers on the same plant,* 37 cts. —— v. aur. varieg.

38 Broad leaved do. —— major

HONEYSUCKLES, 37½ Cents.
Class, *Pentandria.*   Order, *Monogynia.*

1 Striped monthly, *or white fragrant* — Lonicera caprifolium

2 Early sweet Italian —— v. *italica*

3 Early Tartarian —— tartarica

4 English woodbine —— periclymenum

5 Oak leaved —— v. *quercifolium*

6 Variegated oak leaved —— v. *quercifol. varieg.*

7 English fly —— zylosteum

8 Scarlet trumpet, *monthly* — Caprifolium sempervirens

9 Yellow trumpet, $1 —— Fraseri

10 Yellow pubescent, $1 —— pubescens

11 Diervilla, *or Arcadian* — Diervilla lutea

12 Pink azalea, *or American woodbine* — Azalea nudiflora

13 White late flowering do. —— peryclemenoides

14 Double flowering do. $2 —— v. *pleno*

15 Yellow pontic do. $1 —— pontica

ROSES. Rosa.
Class, *Icosandria.* Order, *Polygynia.*

[This favourite flower has been cultivated to such an extent in Europe, that it combines almost every tint of which nature is susceptible, and some of their collections contain above 800 superb varieties. The following have been selected on account of their fragrance, size, beauty, singularity, or delicacy, and the original plants of many of these kinds cost from $1 60 cents to $4 75 cents each, exclusive of the expenses and losses attending importation. A distinct Catalogue of Roses exclusively, containing above 100 other kinds, may be had by amateurs, and it is intended hereafter to keep a permanent stock of 300 select varieties.]

N. B. It may be well to observe that all the following Roses will endure our winters in the open air.

1 Early cinnamon, *or May,* 25 cts.
2 Red officinal, *or conserve,* 25 cts.
3 Dwarf Burgundy, *button, or shell rose,* 37 cts.
4 Crimson velvet, 37 cts.
5 Red   do. 50 cts.
6 Purple   do. *superb,* $1
7 Dark   do. 50 cts.
8 Dark marbled, 50 cts.
9 Moss provence, *red,* $1
10 Blush moss, $1
11 White moss, $5
12 Unique white provence, *superb,* $1 50
13 Childings   do.   75 cts.
14 Royal cabbage   do.   50 cts.
15 Royal Welsh   do. $1
16 Scarlet   do. $1
17 Dutch   do.   75 cts.
18 Common   do.   50 cts.
19 Single   do.   25 cts.
20 Double yellow, $1
21 Double dwarf yellow, $1 50
22 Single yellow, $
23 Straw coloured Scotch, $1 50
24 Yellow and red Austrian, *red above, and yellow beneath,* $1
25 Great maiden's blush, 50 cts.
26 Minor   do.   75 cts.
27 Pompone, *extremely delicate,* $1
28 Rose de Meaux, 50 cts.
29 Blush Belgick, 50 cts.

30 Common white, 37 *cts.*
31 Spineless virgin, *or white thornless,* $1
32 Single red thornless, 25 *cts.*
33 Single blush do. 37 *cts.*
34 Double red do. 75 *cts.*
35 Striped rosa mundi, *or carnation rose,* 50 *cts.*
36 Red damask, 37 *cts.*
37 Dark do. 37 *cts.*
38 Blush do. 37 *cts.*
39 White do. *superb,* 50 *cts.*
40 York and Lancaster, *or Union, divided white and red,* $1
41 Single American sweetbriar, 25 *cts.*
42 ———— European do. *or eglantine,* 25 *cts.*
43 Double red do. $1
44 ———— blush do. $1
45 Semidouble do. 50 *cts.*
46 Yellow do. $1
47 Red monthly, 75 *cts.*
48 Blush do. 75 *cts.*
49 White do. 75 *cts.*
50 Striped do. $1
51 Four seasons, $1
52 Double white musk, *or cluster monthly,* 75 *cts.*
53 Single do. 50 *cts.*
54 Blush musk, *or Champney's monthly,* $1
55 Red musk, 50 *cts.*
56 Multiflora, *or garland rose, a vine flowering in wreaths ; a single plant will cover the side of a large house, and has been known to produce more than ten thousand flowers in a season,* 50 *cts.*
57 Ranunculus, 75 *cts.*
58 Single white Scotch, 25 *cts.*
59 Double white do. 50 *cts.*
60 ———— blush do. 50 *cts.*
61 ———— red do. 50 *cts.*
62 Striped do. 50 *cts.*
63 Great hundred leaved, 37 *cts.*
64 Blush do. 50 *cts.*
65 Singleton's do. 50 *cts.*
66 Blancy's do. 50 *cts.*
67 Petit do. 50 *cts.*
68 Single burnet leaved, 25 *cts.*
69 Double do. 50 *cts.*
70 Single Pennsylvania, 25 *cts.*

71 Double Pennsylvania, *autumn flowering, very delicate,* 50 *cts.*
72 Single Carolina, *or corymbose,* 25 *cts.*
73 Cherokee, *evergreen Georgia, or nondescript,* $1
74 European evergreen, $1
75 White Ayrshire creeper, 50 *cts.*
76 Great royal, 50 *cts.*
77 Blush do. 37 *cts.*
78 Single dog, 37 *cts.*
79 Double do. 75 *cts.*
80 Rose de Juno, $1
81 Belle aurora, 75 *cts.*
82 Aurora brilliante, $1
83 Prolific, *or flos ex flore,* 50 *cts.*
84 Frankfort, *or turban,* 50 *cts.*
85 Transparent, $1
86 Kingston's Portugal, *delicate,* 50 *cts.*
87 St. Francis, *superb,* 50 *cts.*
88 Red mignonne, 75 *cts.*
89 Bicolor do. $1
90 Small do. 75 *cts.*
91 Swiss, $1
92 Spong's, 50 *cts.*
93 Fringe, 75 *cts.*
94 Kingston's new, 75 *cts.*
95 Goliath, 50 *cts.*
96 Giant, 50 *cts.*
97 Hedgehog, *or Russian,* 50 *cts.*
98 Burning coal, *superb,* $1
99 Venerable, 50 *cts.*
100 Dark shell, 75 *cts.*
101 Royal bouquet, 75 *cts.*
102 Perruque, *or wig shaped,* 75 *cts.*
103 Grand pompadour, *extra,* $1
104 Pyramidal, 75 *cts.*
105 Celestial, $1
106 Grand triumphant, $1
107 Grand monarch, $1
108 Carmine, $1
109 Blush gloria mundi, 50 *cts.*
110 Great Mogul, $2
111 King of Rome, $2
112 Lisbon, 75 *cts.*
113 Portland, $1
114 Fiery, $1

E

115 Atlas, 75 *cts.*
116 Nonpareille, $ 1
117 Dutch tree, 75 *cts.*
118 Black mottled, $ 1
119 Early blush, 75 *cts.*
120 Royal do. 75 *cts.*
121 Minor do. 75 *cts.*
122 Imperial do. 75 *cts.*
123 Virgin do. *superb*, $ 1
124 Royal virgin, 50 *cts.*
125 Great purple, 75 *cts.*
126 Bright do. 75 *cts.*
127 Incomparable do. *pourpre incomparable*, $ 1
128 Grand do. 75 *cts.*
129 Fine do. *belle pourpre*, $ 1
130 Royal do. *pourpre royale*, $ 1
131 Triumphant do. *pourpre triomphant*, $ 1
132 Red and violet, *violet et rouge*, 75 *cts.*
133 Royal scarlet, $ 1
134 Stadtholder, 75 *cts.*
135 Rose of Sharon, 50 *cts.*
136 Double apple bearing, 37 *cts.*
137 Brown's fairmaid, 75 *cts.*
138 Emperor, *very dark*, $ 1
139 King, 50 *cts.*
140 Queen, 50 *cts.*
141 Bishop, 50 *cts.*
142 Stæban, 50 *cts.*
143 Rosa blanda, *or Labradore*, $ 1

The following are denominated BLACK ROSES, *on account of their very dark shades.*

144 Black proserpine, $ 1
145 Imperial, *blackest*, $ 1 50
146 Pluto, $ 1
147 Premier noble, $ 1
148 Tuscany, $ 1
149 Negro, $ 1
150 Black, *rose noire*, $ 2
151 Infernal, $ 1
152 Grand Turkey, $ 1
153 Black frizzled, $ 1

NEW FRENCH AND DUTCH ROSES.

$ 1 each, except where noted.

*N. B. The names they are known by in France and Holland
are also annexed.*

154 Triumphant bizarre
155 Red variegated, *Rouge panaché*
156 Admirable do. *Panaché admirable*
157 Incomparable beauty, *Beauté sanspareille*
158 Variegated do. *Beauté panaché*
159 Early do. *Belle hative*, 50 cts.
160 Eastern do. *Beauté orientale*
161 Insurmountable do. *Beauté insurmontable*
162 Unparalleled do. *Belle sanspareille*
163 Variegated bouquet, *Bouquet panaché*
164 Perfect do. *Bouquet parfaite, superb*
165 Favourite agate, *Agathe favorite*
166 Red do. *Rouge agathe*
167 Royal do. *Agathe royale*
168 Incomparable do. *Agathe incomparable*
169 Delicate do. *Mignonne agathe*
170 Crowned rose, *Premier couronné*
171 Great crimson, *Grande cramoisie*
172 Brilliant do. *Cramoisie brilliante*
173 Royal do. *Cramoisie royale*, 75 cts.
174 Incomparable do. *Cramoisie incomparable*
175 Dark violet, *Violet foncé*
176 Delightful do. *Delicieuse violette*
177 Agreeable do. *Violet agréable, superb*
178 Purple do. *Pourpre violette*
179 Lovely do. *Aimable violette*
180 Brilliant do. *Violet brilliant*
181 Incomparable do. *Violet incomparable*
182 Sombre agréable
183 Delicieuse, 75 cts.
184 Imperial superb
185 Brown do. *superb en brun*
186 Delicatesse
187 Admirable, *extra superb*, $ 2
188 Ornement de parade, 75 cts.
189 Bijou de parade, *trinket rose*
190 Fleur de parade, 75 cts.
191 Proserpina regina

192 Agreeable red, *Rouge agréable*
193 Brightest red, *La plus rouge*
194 Dazzling red, *Rouge bien vive*
195 Fine red, *Beau rouge*, 50 cts.
196 Pale red, *Rubro pallido*, 75 cts.
197 Striking red, *Rouge frappante, superb*
198 Glittering red, *Rouge luisante*, 75 cts.
199 Formidable red, *Rouge formidable*, 75 cts.
200 Ornament of the reds, *Ornement des rouges*
201 Glory of the reds, *Gloria rubrorum*
202 King of the reds, *Rex rubrorum*
203 Splendid beauty, *La grande belle*
204 Greatest beauty, *La plus belle*
205 Reddish purple, *Rouge purpureo, superb marbled*
206 Fine   do. *Beau pourpre*, 50 cts.
207 Unrivalled do. *Non plus ultra pourpre*
208 Faultless do. *Pourpre sans defauts*
209 King of the purples, *Roi des pourpres*
210 Purple triumphant, *Pourpre triomphales*
211 Constancy, *La constance*
212 Fashionable, *Premier mode*, 75 cts.
213 Flora's riches, *Riche en fleurs, superb*
214 Greatness, *La grandeur*
215 Great Holland, 75 cts.
216 Heerin rose, 50 cts.
217 Sanspareille
218 Interesting, *L'interessante*, 75 cts.
219 Jolie
220 La palée
221 Lovely, *L'aimable*, 50 cts.
222 Majestic, 75 cts.
223 Marvellous
224 Parisian
225 Précieuse
226 Predominant
227 Predestina
228 Queen of roses, *Reine des roses*
229 Surpassing, *Surpassetout*, 75 cts.
230 White bouquet, *Bouquet blanche*, 75 cts.
231 Royal triumph
232 Superior
233 Triompheronde
234 Thornless alpine
235 Porcelain

CHINESE EVERBLOOMING, OR MONTHLY ROSES.

*N. B. Those marked thus * require a slight covering of straw or litter during winter, the others require no protection.*

236 Chinese pale red, *or daily rose*, 50 cts.
237 ———— blush marbled, *or Hamilton*, 50 cts.
238 *———— purple velvet, *semperflorens, or Otaheite*, 50 cts.
239 ———— blush changeable, *or diversiflora*, $1
240 ———— crimson velvet, $1
241 *———— hundred leaved, $1
242 *———— single velvet, $1
243 ———— rosa odorata, *or tea scented of exquisite fragrance*, $2
244 ———— dwarf, *or pompone, very small and delicate*, $1
245 *———— sanguinea, *deep crimson*, 75 cts.
246 ———— semidouble purple, *variegated*, $1 50
247 *———— bichonia, $1 50
248 *———— resplendent, $1 50
249 *———— lord Macartney's white, $2
250 ———— semidouble lilac, $2
251 *———— amaranthus, $2
252 *———— three leaved, *or rosa sinica*, $2
253 *———— subalba, *red and white*, $1
254 *———— Lawrencia, *the least and most delicate of all roses*, $2

ROSES IN ASSORTMENTS.

The first assortment of 100 Roses of 100 finest kinds, $60
—— second do. do. of 100 fine kinds, $45
—— third do. do. of 50 good kinds, $35

——

PÆONIES.
Class, *Polyandria.* Order, *Digynia.*

1 Single white Turkish, $1	Pæonia albiflora
2 ——— Siberian, $1	——— siberica
3 ——— officinal, $1	——— officinalis *albo*
4 ——— blush, $1	——— v. *albicans*
5 Double white, *or changeable*, $1	——— v. *albicans pleno*

2

6 Single crimson officinal, } Pæonia v. *rubro*
    50 *cts.*
7 Double do. do. 50 *cts.* ——— v. *rubro pleno*
8 Single red   do. 50 *cts.* ——— v. *carnescens*
9 Double do.   do. 50 *cts.* ——— v. *carnescens pleno*
10 Single rose do. 50 *cts.* ——— v. *roseo*
11 Double rose do. 50 *cts.* ——— v. *roseo pleno*
12 Jagged leaved pink co- } ——— anomala
    loured, $ 1
13 Coral coloured, 50 *cts.* ——— corallina
14 Asiatic crimson, $ 1 ——— peregrina
15 Parsley, *or fennel leaved,* $ 1 ——— tenuifolia
16 Double purple fringed, $ 1 ——— paradoxa, *fimbriata*
17 Single dwarf Spanish, $ 1 ——— humilis
18 Double do.   do. $ 1 ——— v. *pleno*
19 Hybrid, *or Mule, violet.* $ 1 ——— hybrida
20 Constantinople purple, } ——— byzantina
    $ 1 50
21 Dauric purple, $ 1 ——— daurica
22 Tartarian, $ 1 50 ——— tartarica
23 Anderson's $ 1 ——— arietina
24 Chinese double crimson, $ 8 ——— Humei
25 ——— double rose scent- } ——— fragrans
    ed, $ 10
26 —— double white, $ 5 ——— Whitleji
27 —— purple tree pæony, $ 5 ——— moutan, *Banksii*
28 —— rose coloured do. $ 5 ——— v. *rosea*
29 —— poppy flowered, $ 25 ——— v. *papaveracea*

An assortment of 20 kinds of Pæonies, $ 15
————————— of 12 kinds of do. $ 9

———

CARNATIONS. Dianthus *caryophyllus.*
Class, *Decandria.* Order, *Monogynia.*

1 Large Red, 37 *cts.* } *These generally measure from*
2 Large rose, 50 *cts.* } *nine to ten inches in cir-*
3 Large white, 37 *cts.* } *cumference.*
4 Rose striped, 50 *cts.*
5 Lilac striped, 50 *cts.*
6 Purple mottled, 37 *cts.*
7 Scarlet, 50 *cts.*

8 Striped tree, 50 *cts.*
9. Wellington rose, *rose leaved*, 50 *cts.*
10 Incomparable, *rose flake, rose leaved,* $1
11 British monarch; *crimson flake, rose leaved,* $1
12 White picotee, 50 *cts.*
13 Orange coloured picotee, 75 *cts.*
14 Pheasant eyed, 37 *cts.*
15 Crimson, 50 *cts.*
16 Purple crimson, 50 *cts.*
17 Velvet crimson, *rose leaved,* $1
18 Small rose, 37 *cts.*
19 Red favourite, 50 *cts.*
20 Flame coloured, 50 *cts.*

N. B. Many new varieties have recently been received from Europe, which will be stated in the next Catalogue.

PINKS, 25 Cents each.

1 Common garden, *many colours*	Dianthus hortensis
2 Wheat ear do.	———— *v. imbricatus*
3 Maiden	———— deltoides
4 China, *or Indian*	———— chinensis
5 Mule, *or hybrid*	———— hybridus
6 Sweet William, *or poetic pink*	———— barbatus
7 Double do.	———— *v. pleno*
8 Fringed	———— superbus
9 Caucasian	———— caucasicus
10 Moss	Phlox subulatus
11 Mountain	Silene pensylvanica

CHINESE CHRYSANTHEMUMS.

Chrysanthemum, *indicum*. Class, *Syngenesia*.
Order, *Superflua*.

50 Cents, except those noted.

[This superb flower (vulgarly denominated Artemesia) is deservedly esteemed; being perfectly hardy, and affording a most brilliant display, at a time when the chilling blasts of autumn have left us but the vestiges of departed verdure. It is therefore a subject of much gratification, that the number known to be cultivated in China exceeds 40 varieties, near 30 of which will be offered to the public in the next Catalogue.]

1 White
2 White quilled
3 Buff changeable, *red and orange flowers on the same plant*
4 Purple
5 Purple quilled
6 Rose coloured
7 Lilac and white, *changeable*, $1
8 Dark crimson
9 Straw coloured
10 Straw coloured quilled, $1
11 Golden yellow, $1

PRIMROSES, POLEANTHUS, AURICULAS, and COWSLIPS. Class, *Pentandria*. Order, *Monogynia*

1 Yellow, *or poetic primrose*, 50 cts.	Primula vulgaris
2 Purple do. 50 cts.	——— v. purpureo
3 Double purple do. $1	——— v. purp. plene
4 Double white do. $1	——— v. albo pleno
5 Double lilac do. $1	——— v. fulva
6 Poleanthus, 25 *varieties*, each 50 cts.	——— polyanthys
7 Double purple do. $1	——— v. purp. plene
8 Auriculas, 20 *varieties*, each 50 cts.	——— auricula
9 Yellow cowslip, 25 cts.	——— veris
10 Purple do. *or hose in hose*, 25 cts.	——— v. purpureo
11 Yellow oxlip, 50 cts.	——— elatior
12 Bird's-eye cowslip, 50 cts.	——— farinosa

IRIS, or *flower de luce*, 25 Cents, except those noted. Class, *Triandria.* Order, *Monogynia.*

[This flower, from its great combination of colours, (whence it derives its name) and altogether unique appearance, has ever found admirers among the curious and the scientific. By the recent addition of a large division of Genus *Morœa*, the number of species has been increased to 55, to which may be added about 30 splendid varieties, which have been raised from seed by the Dutch. Arrangements have been made to import nearly all the other *hardy* species, which will be received the autumn of the present year.]

1 Large purple German	Iris germanica
2 Large two coloured elder scented	⎰ —— sambucina
3 Large white florentine, *or Orris root*, 37 cts.	⎱ —— florentina
4 Great Chalcedonian, *with flowers beautifully mottled, resembling the plumage of an Indian bird*, 50 cts.	—— susiana
5 Naked stalked	—— aphylla
6 Yellow	—— pseudacorus
7 Striped German, 37 *cts.*	—— spuria
8 Variegated Hungarian, *purple and orange*, 50 cts.	—— variegata
9 Purple Virginian	—— virginica
10 Various coloured	—— versicolor
11 Prismatic	—— prismatica
12 Red flowering, 37 *cts.*	—— cuprœa
13 Blue Carolina, 37 *cts.*	—— tridentata
14 Dwarf vernal, 37 *cts.*	—— verna
15 Dwarf crested	—— cristata
16 Dwarf purple Austrian	—— pumila
17 Snake's head, 50 *cts.*	—— tuberosa
18 Chinese fringed, $1	—— chinensis
19 Siberian, 50 *cts.*	—— sibirica
20 Striped leaved, $1	—— fœtidissima, *varieg.*
21 Grass leaved, 37 *cts.*	—— graminea
22 Slender leaved, 37 *cts.*	—— tenuifolia
23 Twice flowering, 37 *cts.*	—— biflora
24 Forked, 37 *cts.*	—— dichotoma
25 Brown flowered, 50 *cts.*	—— squalens

26 Persian
27 Peacock
28 Spanish bulbous
29 Double flowering do.
30 English bulbous

} for 30 superb varieties, see Bulbous flowers. {

Iris persica
—— pavonia
—— xiphium
—— v. *pleno*
—— xiphioides

An assortment of 20 species of Iris $ 6

HEMEROCALLIS, or *Day Lily.*
Class, *Hexandria.* Order, *Monogynia.*

1 Bright yellow, 25 *cts.*   Hemerocallis flava
2 Red, *or copper coloured,* 25cts. —— —— fulva
3 Double do. $ 1.   —————— v. *pleno*
4 Blue Japanese, 50 *cts.*   ————— cærulea
5 White do. *splendid,* $ 2   ————— japonica
6 Siberian grass leaved, $ 1 ————— graminea
7 Chinese fan-like, $ 1   ————— disticha

HERBACEOUS PERENNIAL PLANTS,
25 Cents, except those noted.

1 St. Bruno's lily, 50 *cts.*   Anthericum liliastrum
2 Grass leaved anthericum,
   50 *cts.* } ————— liliago
3 Scarlet Columbine   Aquilegia canadensis
4 European blue do.   ————— vulgaris
5 Purple do.   ————— v. *purp.*
6 White do.   ————— v. *albo*
7 Red do.   ————— v. *rubro*
8 Double starry do. 50 *cts.* ————— v *pleno*
9 Striped do. *beautiful,* 50 *cts.* ————— hybrida
10 Upright birthwort, 50 *cts.* Aristolochia clematitis
11 European reed, 50 *cts.* Arundo phragmites
12 Ribband grass   ————— v. *striata*
13 Orange coloured swallow-
   wort } Asclepias tuberosa
14 Red do.   ————— incarnata
15 Hairy leaved do.   ————— var. *pulchra*

16 White swallowwort	Asclepias verticillata
17 Yellow asphodel, *or king's spear,* 50 cts.	Asphodelus luteus
18 White do.	———— ramosus
19 Aster, *many species*	Aster, *sp.*
20 Mountain daisy	Bellis perennis
21 Double red do.	—— hortensis
22 Red quilled do.	—— *v. fistulosa*
23 White do. 50 cts.	—— *v. alba*
24 White quilled do. 50 *cts.*	—— ————*fistulosa*
25 Blush quilled do. 50 *cts.*	—— *v. carnea*
26 Variegated do.	—— *v. variegata*
27 Hen and chicken do. 50 *cts.*	—— *v. prolifera*
28 Prickly pear, *or Indian fig,* 50 cts.	Cactus opuntia
29 Great bellflower, *or throat-wort,* 50 cts.	Campanula trachelium
30 Syrian do.	———— mollis
31 Betony leaved do.	———— betonicifolia
32 Maryland cassia	Cassia marylandica
33 Blue catananche, 50 cts.	Catananche cærulea
34 New-Jersey tea, *delicate,* 50 *cts.*	Ceanothus americanus
35 White chelone	Chelone glabra
36 Black snake root	Cimicifuga serpentaria
37 Brown flowering clematis, 37 *cts.*	Clematis ochroleuca
38 Austrian entire leaved do. 50 *cts.*	—— integrifolia
39 Upright do. 50 *cts.*	———— erecta
40 Lily of the valley	Convallaria majalis
41 Solomon's seal	———— racemosa
42 Rose coloured perennial convolvulus	Convolvulus sepium
43 Large white do. 50 cts.	———— panduratus
44 Double white do. $1	———— *v. pleno*
45 Officinal jalap, 50 *cts.*	———— jalapa
46 Palmated coreopsis	Coreopsis tripteris
47 Superb do. 50 *cts.*	———— tinctoria
48 Great flowering do. 50 *cts.*	———— grandiflora
49 Yellow lady's slipper, 50 *cts.*	Cypripedium pubescens
50 White and red splendid do. 75 *cts.*	———— spectabile
51 Red do. 37 *cts.*	———— humile

52 European yellow do. $1	Cypripedium calceolus
53 Siberian bee larkspur	Delphinium elatum
54 Large flowering do.	————— grandiflorum
55 Double flowering do. $1	————— v. pleno
56 Azure blue do. 50 cts.	————— azureum
57 White Fraxinella. This plant exhales inflammable gas, 50 cts.	Dictamnus alba
58 Red do. 50 cts.	————— v. rubra
59 Virginian dragon's head	Dracocephalum virginicum
60 Narrow leaved epilobium, 50 cts.	Epilobium angustifolium
61 Yucca leaved eryngo, 37 cts.	Eryngium yuccifolium
62 Flat leaved do. 50 cts.	————— planum
63 Blue eupatorium, beautiful	Eupatorium caelestinum
64 Purple do.	————— purpureum
65 Trifoliate do. and many others	————— trifoliatum
66 Soapwort gentian	Gentiana saponaria
67 Crosswort do.	————— cruciata
68 Yellowish do.	————— ochroleuca
69 Catesby's do.	————— Catesbæi
70 Bloody geranium	Geranium sanguineum
71 Blue do	————— maculatum
72 Double Scotch do. 50 cts.	————— sylvaticum, pleno
73 Striped flowered do.	————— striatum
74 Yellow gerardia, splendid, 37 cts	Gerardia quercifolia
75 Autumnal flowering helenium	Helenium autumnale
76 Perennial sunflower	Helianthus divaricatus
77 Tallest do.	————— altissimus
78 Narrow leaved do.	————— angustifolius
79 Silvery leaved do.	————— canescens
80 Rose coloured hibiscus	Hibiscus palustris
81 White and purple ditto, splendid, 37 cts.	————— moscheutos
82 Halbert leaved do. 37 cts.	————— militaris
83 Sweet seneca grass	Holcus odoratus
84 Largest St. John's-wort, 37 cts.	Hypericum ascyroides
85 Rose coloured perennial pea	Lathyrus latifolius
86 Scarlet cardinal flower	Lobelia cardinalis
87 Blue lobelia	————— siphilitica
88 Crimson do. 50 ts.	————— fulgens
89 Splendid do. $1	————— splendens
90 Blue perennial lupin	Lupinus perennis

91 Yellow perennial lupin, 50 *cts.* } Lupinus nootkatensis
92 Scarlet lychnis   Lychnis chalcedonica
93 Double scarlet do. *very splendid*, 50 *cts.* } ———— *v. pleno*
94 Willow herb, 50 *cts.*   Lythrum salicaria
95 Carolina reed, 50 *cts.*   Miegia macrosperma
96 Delicate mimosa, *beauti-ful*, 50 *cts.* } Mimosa illinoensis
97 Blue monkey flower   Mimulus ringens
98 Crimson monarda   Monarda didyma
99 Yellow do.   ———— punctata
100 Pale purple do.   ———— oblongata
101 Pale red do.   ———— fistulosa
102 White do.   ———— gracilis
103 Forget-me-not   Myosotis arvensis
104 Oriental poppy, 50 *cts.*   Papaver orientale
105 Blackberry lily   Pardanthus chinensis
106 Red phlox, *or lychnadea*   Phlox paniculata
107 Purple spotted do.   ——— maculata
108 Wave leaved do.   ——— undulata
109 White do.   ——— suaveolens
110 Pale red do.   ——— subulata
111 Purple everlasting pea   Pisum maritimum
112 May apple, *or wild man-drake* } Podophyllum peltatum
113 Blue Greek valerian, 37 *cts.* Polemonium ceruleum
114 Double feverfew, 37 *cts.* Pyrethrum parthenium
115 Double yellow ranuncu-lus, 50 *cts.* } Ranunculus acris, *pl.*
116 Double white do. *or fair-maids of France*, 75 *cts.* } ——— aconitifolius, *pl.*
117 Dyer's madder   Rubia tinctorium
118 Purple rudbeckia   Rudbeckia purpurea
119 Jagged leaved yellow do. ——— lasciniata
120 Hairy leaved yellow do. ——— hirta
121 Three lobed do.   ——— triloba
122 White officinal soapwort Saponaria officinalis
123 Double white do.   ——— *v. pleno*
124 Double rose coloured do. ——— *v. roseo*
125 Purple side saddle flower, 50 *cts.* } Sarracenia purpurea
126 Yellow do. 50 *cts.*   ——— flava

F

127 Purple Siberian saxi-} Saxifraga crassifolia
    frage, 50 *cts.*
128 Granulated do. ——— granulata
129 Chrysanthemum leaved} Scrophularia chrysanthemifolia
    scrophularia
130 European scullcap Scutellaria rubicunda
131 Live-for-ever, *or ever-*} Sedum anacampseros
    green orpine
132 Yellow flowering stone-} ——— aizoon
    crop
133 Neat flowering do ———pulchellum
134 Purslane leaved do. ——— ternatum
135 Poplar leaved do. ——— populifolium
136 Smooth leaved sida Sida napæa
137 Palmated do. ——— dioica
138 Blue sophora Sophora cærulea
139 White do. ——— alba
140 Yellow do. *To this* }
    plant flies have such an
    aversion, that they will } ——— tinctoria
    quickly leave the spot
    where it is placed
141 Siberian do. ——— lupinoides
142 Medicinal pink root, 50*cts.* Spigelia marylandica
143 Double meadow sweet Spiræa ulmaria, *pl.*
144 Double dropwort. ——— filipendula, *pl.*
145 Red Siberian spiræa ——— lobata
146 Goat's beard do. 50 *cts.* ——— aruncus
147 Thrift, *or sea pink* Statice armeria
148 Blue Virginian spider-} Tradescantia virginica
    wort
149 Pale blue do. 37 *cts.* ——— *v. pallida*
150 White do. 50 *cts.* ——— *v. alba*
151 Rose coloured do. 50 *cts.* ——— rosea
152 European globe flower,} Trollius europæus
    50 *cts.*
153 Asiatic do. 50 *cts.* ——— asiaticus
154 Rose coloured vervain Verbena aubletia
155 Scarlet valerian Valeriana rubra
156 White do. ———*v. alba*
157 Garden do. ——— phu
158 Green American helle-} Veratrum viride
    bore
159 Purple autumnal vernonia Vernonia noveboracensis

160 Virginian speedwell, *ce-lebrated for cures of dropsy, leprosy, and salt-rheum, 50 cts. or a quantity with prescrip-tion, $3* } Veronica virginica

161 Blue fragrant violet, 12 cts.   Viola odorata
162 Double blue do.   —— *v. pleno*
163 Double purple do.   —— *v. purpurea pleno*
164 Bird's foot do. 12 cts.   —— pedata
165 Palmated do. 12 cts.   —— palmata
166 Adam's thread, *or thready yucca,* 50 cts. } Yucca filamentosa

———

MEDICINAL and CULINARY EXOTICS,
Biennial and Perennial, 12 to 25 Cents each, except those noted.

1 Sneezewort   Achillea ptarmica
2 Water plantain   Alisma plantago
3 Chives   Allium schnænoprasum
4 Common garlick   ——— sativum
5 Marsh mallow   Althæa officinalis
6 Sweet alyssum   Alyssum maritimum
7 Officinal bugloss   Anchusa officinalis
8 Dill   Anethum graveolens
9 Finochio   ——— *v. ozoricum*
10 Fennel   ——— fœniculum
11 Garden angelica   Angelica archangelica
12 Shining angelica   ——— triquinata
13 Chamomile   Anthemis nobilis
14 Smallage   Apium graveolens
15 Burdock   Arctium lappa
16 Snake root   Aristolochia sempervirens
17 Wormwood   Artemesia absinthium
18 Tarragon, *or astragon*   ——— dracunculus
19 Asarabacca   Asarum canadense
20 Black swallowwort, 37 cts.   Asclepias nigra
21 Deadly nightshade, 50 cts.   Atropa belladona
22 Mandrake, 50 cts.   ——— mandragora
23 Officinal betony   Betonica officinalis

24 Officinal borage	Borago officinalis
25 Caraway	Carum carui
26 Celandine	Chelidonium majus
27 Wild succory	Chicorium intybus
28 Poisonous cicuta	Cicuta maculata
29 Horse radish	Cochlearia armoracia
30 Poison hemlock	Conium maculatum
31 Coriander	Coriandrum sativum
32 Sea kale	Crambe maritima
33 Garden artichoke	Cynara scolymus
34 Cardoon	——— cardunculus
35 Purple fox glove	Digitalis purpurea
36 White do.	——— v. alba
37 Fuller's teazel	Dipsacus fullonium
38 Wild do.	——— sylvestris
39 Caper spurge	Euphorbia lathyris
40 Officinal goat's rue	Galega officinalis
41 European liquorice, 50 cts.	Glycirrhiza glabra
42 Green hellebore, 50 cts.	Helleborus viridis
43 Black do. or Christmas rose, 50 cts.	——— niger
44 Jerusalem artichoke	Helianthus tuberosus
45 Sweet rocket	Hesperis matronalis
46 Common hop	Humulus lupulus
47 Black henbane	Hyoscyamus niger
48 Officinal hyssop	Hyssopus officinalis
49 Elecampane	Inula helenium
50 Dyer's woad	Isatis tinctoria
51 Common lavendar	Lavandula spica
52 Dandelion	Leontodon taraxacum
53 Motherwort	Leonurus cardiaca
54 Lovage	Ligusticum levisticum
55 Horehound	Marrubium vulgare
56 Common balm	Melissa officinalis •
57 Peppermint	Mentha piperita
58 Spearmint	——— viridis
59 Catmint, or nep	Nepeta cataria
60 Common marjoram	Origanum vulgare
61 Ginseng	Panax quinquefolium
62 Common winter cherry	Physalis alkekengi
63 Anise	Pimpinella anisum
64 Common burnet	Poterium sanguisorba
65 Great self-heal	Prunella grandiflora
66 Officinal lungwort	Pulmonaria officinalis

67 Tart rhubarb, 50 cts.	Rheum undulatum
68 Turkey do. 50 cts.	——— rhaponticum
69 Officinal do. 50 cts.	——— palmatum
70 Tartarian do. 50 cts.	——— tartaricum
71 Thick leaved do. $1	——— compactum
72 Garden patience dock	Rumex patientia
73 Garden sorrel	——— acetosa
74 Common rue	Ruta graveolens
75 Officinal sage	Salvia officinalis
76 Clary	——— sclarea
77 Officinal, or field burnet	Sanguisorba officinalis
78 Canadian burnet	——————— canadensis
79 Puccoon, or blood root	Sanguinaria canadensis
80 Sweet scabious	Scabiosa atropurpurea
81 Myrrh, or sweet sicely	Scandix odorata
82 Scrophulary	Scrophularia marylandica
83 Officinal scullcap	Scutellaria lateriflora
84 Common house leek	Sempervivum tectorum
85 Water cress	Sisymbrium officinalis
86 Skirret	Sium sirsarum
87 Trifoliate spiræa	Spiræa trifoliata
88 Comfrey	Symphytum officinale
89 Oriental do.	——————— orientale
90 Tansy	Tanacetum vulgare
91 Common thyme	Thymus vulgaris
92 Lemon do.	——— serpyllum
93 Fenugreek	Trigonella fœnumgræcum
94 Common colt's foot	Tussilago farfara
95 Butter bur	——————— petassites

BIENNIAL and PERENNIAL EXOTIC FLOWERS, 12 to 25 Cents each, except those noted.

1 Rose campion	Agrostemma coronaria
2 China hollyhock, various colours	Althæa rosea
3 Double yellow do.	——— v. flava pleno
4 Black do.	——— v. nigra
5 Scarlet snap dragon	Antirrhinum majus
6 Canterberry bell	Campanula medium

f 2

7 Scotch thistle	Carduus eriophorus
8 Bladder campion	Cucubalus behen
9 Starry do.	———— stellatus
10 Great globe thistle	Echinops sphærocephalus
11 Spongy flowered fumitory	Fumaria fungosa
12 Musk geranium	Geranium moschatum
13 French honeysuckle	Hedysarum coronarium
14 Perennial flax	Linum perenne
15 Honesty, *or satin leaf*	Lunaria biennis
16 Diœcious lychnis	Lychnis dioica
17 White upright reseda	Reseda alba
18 London pride	Saxifraga umbrosa
19 Woolly leaved stachys	Stachys lanata
20 Heart's-ease, *or pansey*	Viola tricolor

ANNUAL FLOWERS.

Several hundred species are cultivated in the Garden, but they are of so little moment, that it would be superfluous to give their names in detail.

BULBOUS

AND

FIBROUS ROOTED PLANTS.

— — —

The following have been selected with great care from the finest collections in Holland, and are remarkable for their size, beauty, or delicacy; they are cultivated under the same names by which they were imported, and the prices of many of them are less than the retail prices in Holland, the proprietor relying on the increase for remuneration.

‡ denotes extra fine sorts.
† ———— the earliest sorts.
* ———— those that are tender.

DOUBLE HYACINTHS.
Hyacinthus *orientalis.*
Class, *Hexandria.* Order, *Monogynia.*

Deep Red and Crimson.

	Each. $ cts	Dozen. $ cts
1 ‡Amelia Galotti	25	3
2 ‡Augustus rex	75	6
3 †Beauté suprème	50	4
4 ‡Betty	1 50	12
5 †Boerhaave	37	3 25
6 †Bouquet formé	50	4 50
7 Charlotte Mortimer	37	3
8 Count Bathiany	25	2 50
9 ‡Count de la Coste	1	8
10 Couronne d'or	50	4 50
11 ‡Delice de flore	50	4 50
12 †Delice du printems	50	4 50
13 ‡†Diadème de flore	25	3
14 ‡Dutchess de Parma	50	4

	Each.	Dozen.
	$ cts	$ cts
15 ††Flos sanguineas	25	2 50
16 La beauté suprème	50	4
17 ‡La fidelle	25	2 50
18 La victoire	1	8
19 ‡L'opulence	75	6
20 ††Madame Zoutman	50	4
21 Marquis de la Coste	75	6
22 Pileus cardinalis	25	2 50
23 Princesse Autrichienne	1	8
24 ‡Rex rubrorum	50	4 50
25 Rouge bordé vert, *red and green*	50	4
26 Rouge charmante	31	3
27 †Soleil brillant	25	2 50
28 ‡Viscountess d'Hereria	1	8
Finest reds, 50 *varieties by name*		3
Fine reds, 100 *varieties mixed*	25	1 50

Pale Red and Rosy.

	Each.	Dozen.
29 ‡Beauté brilliante	1	8
30 Beauté honteuse	50	4
31 ‡Betty	1 25	12
32 †Charlotte de Montmorency	25	2 50
33 Favorite des dames	50	4
34 ‡Gloriosa superba	62	6
35 ‡Groot voorst, *grand duke*	50	4 50
36 Habit nuptial	37	3 50
37 †Hugo grotius	25	2 50
38 †Julia	25	2 50
39 La magnifique	25	2 50
40 ‡L'honneur d'Amsterdam	62	6
41 Lord Cochrane	50	4
42 ‡Marquis de Bonacque	37	3 25
43 Rose virginale	50	4
44 Rose surpassante	25	2 50
45 Rose sceptre	50	4 50
46 Temple of Diana	25	2 50
47 ‡Temple of Apollo	37	3 25
Finest rosy, &c. 40 *varieties by name*		3
Fine do. 75 *varieties mixed*	25	1 50

Purple and Dark Blue.

	Each. $ cts	Dozen. $ cts
48 Attilla	37	3
49 Bailif d'Amstelland	25	2 50
50 Bleu Foncé	25	2 50
51 †Cæruleus imperialis	31	3
52 Charmante violette	25	2 50
53 ‡Commandant	50	4 50
54 Count Van Beuren	25	2 50
55 ‡Count d'Ovelliers	50	4 50
56 ‡Datames	50	4 50
57 ‡Dutchess of Normandy	50	4
58 Emperor Titus	25	3
59 Emperor Tiberius	25	2 50
60 Flos ex flore	25	2
61 Fontainebleau	31	3
62 ‡Globe céleste	62	6
63 Habit Romain	25	2 50
64 ‡Jupiter	75	6
65 King's spear	50	2 50
66 King Aginsarus	25	2
67 Kroon des Mooren	25	2
68 †La bien aimé	25	3
69 †‡L'amitié	31	6
70 ‡La majestueuse	75	2 50
71 Linnæus	25	4 50
72 Marshal de France	50	2 50
73 ‡Martinet	50	4 50
74 †Mon ami	25	2 50
75 †‡ Negros superbe	50	4 50
76 Nigritienne	37	3
77 Pluto	25	2 50
78 Pourpre imperiale	31	3
79 Roi Baleus	25	2
80 ‡Roi des bleues	62	6
81 ‡Superbe en noir	50	4 50
82 Susanna Elizabeth	75	6
83 Tyrian purple	37	3
84 Velours noir	50	4 50
85 †‡Velours pourpre	50	4 50
Finest purples, &c. 60 *varieties by name*		3
Fine do. and do. 100 *varieties by name*	25	1 50

Pale Blue and Porcelaine.

	Each.	Dozen.
	$ cts	$ cts
86 ††Admiral de Ruyter	25	2 50
87 †A-la-mode	31	3
88 ‡Belle agathe	25	3
89 ††Bucentaurus	31	3
90 ‡Captain general	62	6
91 ‡Count Bentick	75	6
92 ‡Count de St. Priest	1	8
93 Diodemus	31	3
94 Dome d'Utrecht	37	3 25
95 †Duke d'Anjou	25	2 50
96 Flora	37	3 25
97 ‡Globe terreste	37	3
98 ‡Gloria florum	25	2 50
99 Grande merveilleuse	25	2 50
100 Grand treasurer of Britain	25	2 50
101 ‡Grand-sultan	25	2 50
102 ‡Habit brilliant	50	4 50
103 Incomparable azure	25	2 50
104 ‡L'abbe de Veirac	75	8
105 La rosée	37	3 25
106 ‡Monsieur	62	6
107 Nouvelle mode	50	4 50
108 Oldenbarnweld	25	2
109 ‡Pasquin	50	4 50
110 ††Passetout	25	2 50
111 ‡Prince Henry de Prusse	37	3 25
112 Representant	25	2
113 Robinson	25	3
114 States general	25	3
Finest pale blues, &c. 40 *varieties by name*		3
Fine do. 50 *varieties mixed*	25	1 50

White, and White with Yellow Eyes.

	Each.	Dozen.
115 Aimable blanche	50	4 50
116 Andromeda	31	3
117 Concordia	75	6
118 Countess de Rechters	37	3
119 Don gratuit	25	3
120 ‡Dutchess of Berry	37	3
121 Dutchess of Bedford	25	2 50

		Each.	Dozen.
		$ cts	$ cts
122	Dulcinea	25	2 50
123	Flavo superbe	31	3
124	‡Gloria florum	25	2 50
125	Grand triumph	25	2 50
126	Illustre pyramidale	31	3
127	Infant princess	25	2 50
128	Jeannette	75	6
129	Labien aimé	25	2 50
130	Liberté d'or	25	2 50
131	Margrave of Baden	25	3
132	†Marmontel	50	4
133	Minerva	25	2 50
134	Nannette	31	3
135	Saturnus	62	6
136	Sceptre d'or	50	4 50
137	‡Sultan Achmet	50	4 50
138	‡Suprema alba	1	8
139	‡Viscountesse de Dogenfield	37	3
140	Virgo	25	3
141	Yellow eye	25	2 50
	40 finest varieties *by name*		3
	60 fine do. *mixed*	25	1 50

White, with Red and Pink Eyes.

		Each.	Dozen.
142	††Admiral Zoutman	37	3
143	‡American Congress	75	8
144	Anna Maria	1	8
145	Belle blanche incarnate	25	2 50
146	‡Belle forme	37	3 50
147	Diana of Ephesus	62	6
148	††Duke of Berry	25	2 50
149	‡Furius Camillus	1	9
150	General Washington	1	10
151	‡Gloria florum suprema	75	6
152	†Illustre beauté	31	3
153	Jewel of Harlaem	25	2 50
154	‡Juno	50	5
155	King Solomon	50	4 50
156	La belle nouailles	25	2 50
157	†Madame de St. Simon	50	4 50
158	‡Montgolfier	50	5

	Each.	Dozen.
	$ cts	$ cts
159 ⸸Og, king of Basan	25	2 50
160 Prince Guillaume Frederick	50	4 50
30 finest *varieties by name*		3
40 fine do. *mixed*	25	1 50

White, with Violet and Purple Eyes.

	Each.	Dozen.
161 ⸸Bailif de Zuidwyk	50	4 50
162 Beauté tendre	50	4 50
163 ⸸⸸Bijoux des amateurs	50	4
164 ⸸Candidus violaceus	37	3
165 ⸸⸸Cœur aimable	25	2 50
166 Cœur noir	50	2 50
167 Constantia Elizabeth	25	2 50
168 ⸸Dr. Franklin	50	4 50
169 Ersprins	62	6
170 ⸸⸸Flavus Josephus	50	4
171 La cherie	31	3
172 ⸸Miss Kitty, *largest*	2 50	25
173 Paris de Marmontel	25	2 50
174 Pope Pius	50	4 -
175 ⸸Sphera mundi	62	6
176 States general	50	4 50
177 ⸸Violet superbe	50	4 50
40 finest *varieties by name*		3
50 fine do. *mixed*	25	1 50

Yellow and Orange with various Eyes.

	Each.	Dozen.
178 Anna Pawlowna, *semidouble*	1 50	12
179 Anton, *semidouble*	75	6
180 ⸸Bouquet orange	1	9
181 Chrysolore	50	4 50
182 ⸸Duc de Berry d'or	50	4 50
183 ⸸Grand Alexander, *extra*	2 50	20
184 Jaune constante	1	9
185 Jaune inconstante	50	4 50
186 La favorite	1	10
187 L'or d'Espagne	1	10
188 L'or d'Peru, *extra*	2 50	20
189 ⸸L'or vegetable	37	3
190 Louis d'or	50	3
191 Ophir	25	2 50

	Each.	Dozen.
	$ cts	$ cts
193 Pure d'or	1 25	12
194 Pyramide jaune	50	4 50
195 Vainqueur	1 25	12
20 finest varieties *by name*		6
25 fine do. *mixed*	31	3
Inferior *mixed*	25	2

SINGLE HYACINTHS.

Rosy and Crimson.

196 Acteur	25	2 50
197 Aimable Rozette	25	2 50
198 Belle Hollandoise	25	2 50
199 ‡Diademe de flore	25	2 50
200 ‡Henrietta Wilhelmina	50	5 50
201 ‡L'eclair, *deepest crimson*	1 50	15
202 ‡Paix d'Amiens, *crimson, extra*	1	9
203 ‡Princess of Esterhazy, *crimson, extra*	62	6
204 ‡Raphael	75	8
205 ‡Theodora Wilhelmina	50	4 50
25 varieties *by name*		3
40 do. *mixed*	25	1 50

Blue and Purple.

206 ‡Appius	50	4 50
207 Belle porcelaine	25	2 50
208 Boas	27	3
209 Buonaparte	50	4 50
210 Bonté held	50	4
211 Ceruleus imperialis	25	2 50
212 Charmante bonté	25	2 50
213 Charmante pourpre	25	2 50
214 Count Van Buren	25	2 50
215 Crepiscule	37	3
216 ‡Emilius	25	2 50
217 Emicus	50	4 50
218 Joab	25	2
219 La grandeur	25	2
220 L'ami du cœur, *darkest*	50	4 50
221 Lucina	25	2
222 Lord Nelson	25	2 50
223 Orondates	25	2

	Each.	Dozen.
	$ cts	$ cts
224 ‡Parfait bouquet	37	3 50
225 Pausanias	25	2 50
226 Perle de France	31	3 50
227 Perruque noir	50	4 50
228 †Pronkjuweel	37	3
229 Vainqueur	37	3 50
40 varieties *by name*		2 50
40 do. *mixed*	25	1 50

White.

230 Belle Galathé	25	2 50
231 ‡Grand blanche imperiale	25	2 50
232 Grandeur triumphant	25	2 50
233 Monarque du monde	50	4 50
234 †‡Premier noble	25	2 50
235 Pyramide superbe	25	2 50
236 ‡Roi de Basan	62	5
237 Seconde imperiale	25	2 50
238 Triumph blandina	31	3
20 varieties *by name*		2 50
25 do. *mixed*	25	1 50

Yellow.

239 Adonia	25	2 50
240 Beauté jaune	25	2
241 Couronne Van Audan	25	2 50
242 Goudemunt	37	3
243 Jaune tendre	2,5	2
244 Jonquille	50	4 50
245 Pluie d'or	25	2 50
246 Prince d'Orange	31	3
247 Toison d'or	25	2 50
248 Vorst Van Dessau	37	3
12 varieties *by name*		2 50
20 do. *mixed*	25	1 50

HYACINTHS—*Different Species.*

249 Blue grape hyacinth	Hyacinthus botryoides	12	1
250 Purple grape	——— *v. purpureo*	15	1 50
251 White grape	——— *v. albo*	15	1 50
252 Pale blue grape	——— *v. pallido*	15	1 50

		Each. $ cts	Dozen. $ cts
253 Tassel, *or two coloured* Hyacinthus comosus		25 2	
254 ‡Large feathered	———— monstrosus	25 2	
255 Musk, *or nutmeg*	———— muscari	25 1 50	
256 Large do.	———— *v. major*	25 2	
257 Blue harebells	———— nonscriptus	12 1	
258 Small blue do.	———— *v. cerul.min.*	12 1	
259 White do.	———— *v. albo*	20 1 50	
260 Rose do.	———— *v. roseo*	20 1 50	
261 Red do.	———— *v. rubro*	20 1 50	
262 Violet do.	———— *v. violaceo*	20 1 50	
263 Cluster flowered	———— racemosus	12 1	

HYACINTHS—*By Assortments.*

The first assortment of 100 Hyacinths, *of 100 exquisite double varieties, one of each by name* $ 35

The second assortment of 100 do. *of 50 fine double varieties, two of each by name* 25

The third assortment of 100 do. *of 25 good double varieties, four of each by name* 20

The fourth assortment of 100 do. *of 20 varieties, five of each by name* 15

Various kinds, *mixed*, per 100 12

TULIP. Tulipa *gesneriana.*
Class, *Hexandria.* Order, *Monogynia.*

Early Tulips.

These are of every shade, and begin blooming about two weeks before any of the others.

	Each. $ cts	Dozen. $ cts
1 Aspasia	25 2	
2 ‡Bizar blyhof	25 2	
3 ——— verdiset	25 2	
4 ——— plaisante, *producing often several flowers on one stalk*	37 3	
5 ‡——— pronkert	50 3 50	
6 ——— d'Allemagne	50 4	
7 Bruid de Harlaém	25 2	

No.	Name	Each $ cts	Dozen $ cts
		25	2
8	Brun pourpre	37	3
9	Cerise panaché	50	4 50
10	†——— rectifié, *extra*	25	2
11	‡Clairmonde	25	2
12	————— seconde	25	2
13	————— goude	25	2
14	Count Holstein	25	2
15	Couronne flammé	25	2
16	Cramoisie royale	25	2
17	————— superbe	50	4 50
18	————— de Baden, *rectifié*	25	2
19	Damiathe blanche	25	2
20	Drapeau	25	1 75
21	Duke Van Thol	50	4
22	——— ———, *white*	25	2
23	——— Van Harlaem	25	2
24	——— Voorhelm	25	2
25	——— Orange	25	2
26	——— de Holstein	25	2 50
27	——— de Wurtemburg	25	2
28	——— Bennebroek	25	2
29	——— Victor	25	2
30	Drap d'or	25	2
31	Feu de Moscow	25	2 50
32	——— d'Aboukir	25	2
33	——— de l'Empire, *striped leaved*	25	2
34	Graaf florus	25	2
35	Grand maitre de Maltha	25	2
36	Hecuba	25	2
37	Hof Van Brabant	25	2
38	Isabella	25	2
39	Jason	25	2
40	La belle alliance	25	2
41	Lac bon flos, *striped leaved*	25	2
42	Lac met bontloff	37	3
43	Le brilliant	25	2
44	Manasse	25	2
45	Ma plus aimable	25	2
46	Marquis de Westenrade	25	2
47	Milthiades, *pure white*	25	2
48	Minerva	25	2
49	Paars Morlion, *rectifié*		

	Each.	Dozen.
	$ cts	$ cts
50 Paragon Yzerhand	25	2
51 ——— gulde bloem	25	2
52 ——— Brandson	25	2
53 Pavillon de flore	25	2
54 Pottebaker	25	2
55 Prince Starrenberg	25	2
56 Princess	25	2
57 Reine Esther	25	2
58 Rose merveille	25	2 50
59 Ruban d'or	25	1 75
60 ‡Standard royal	25	2
61 Thomas Moore	25	2
62 Ulysses	25	2
63 Vurige feu	37	3
64 Vuurberg	25	2
65 Wapen Van Leyden, *Leyden Arms*	25	1 75
66 Waterloo	25	2
67 White swan	25	2
68 White bordered red	25	2
69 Yellow and red Van Leyden	25	2
75 finest varieties *by name*	25	2
100 fine do. *mixed*	20	1 50

Bizarre Tulips.

These are violet, purple, brown, red, and rose co-loured, and all intermediate shades on yellow grounds.

	Each.	Dozen.
70 Abbadon	37	3 50
71 Abbé de St. Omer	50	4
72 African, *striped leaved*	37	3
73 ‡Anacreon	50	4 50
74 Aquivera	37	3
75 Archidalia	50	4
76 Aurora borealis	50	4
77 Baron de Reischach	25	2
78 ‡Beauté parfaite	50	4
79 Brigitte	25	2 50
80 Carigula	50	4
81 Charbonnier noir	62	6
82 ‡Duke of Richmond	25	2
83 ‡Electeur de Cologne	37	3 50

	Each. $ cts	Dozen. $ cts
84 Estimée	25 2	
85 Fredericus Rex	25 2	
86 ‡General Daun	25 2	
87 Gloire de France	25 2	
88 ‡Gloria mundi	1	9
89 Goliah	37 3	
90 ‡Gordianus	62 6	
91 Goudheurs	50 4	
92 Grand duke	25 2	
93 ‡Grand Monarque	1	9
94 ‡Grand triumph	50 4	50
95 Incomparable primus	50 4	
96 La beauté fine	25 2	
97 L'eveille	50 4	
98 La reine	25 2	
99 L'Autrichien	62 6	
100 Le dæuil, *or devil*	50 4	
101 ‡Madagascar	50 4	50
102 ‡Mandello	50 4	50
103 Metropolitan	25 2	
104 Miroir	25 2	
105 Monsieur Badier	75 6	
106 Nabob	25 2	
107 Non plus ultra, *extra*	2 50 20	
108 Nouveau triumphant	25 2	
109 ‡Pain d'epices	25 2	
110 Perfecta	75 6	
111 Pont d'Arcole, *extra*	1 25 12	
112 Pourpre de Tyre	50 4	
113 Reine de France	25 2	
114 Rex indiarum	50 4	
115 Roi d'Hollande, *extra*	1 25 20	
116 Sans mère, *very large*	50 4	50
117 Semiramus	37 4	
118 ‡Semper Augustus. *This Tulip sold during the Tulip-mania in Holland, for $ 4000*	1	9
119 Struisvogel	75 6	
120 ‡Tige rouge,	50 4	50
121 Valentienne	75 6	
122 ‡Yellow crown	37 3	
60 finest varieties *by name*	2	
100 fine do. *mixed*	20 1 50	

Bibloem Tulips.

These are black, purple, violet, and brown, and all intermediate shades, on white grounds.

	Each. $ cts	Dozen. $ cts
123 Clovis	25	2
124 Croonvogel	25	2
125 Duc de Boufleurs	25	2
126 Grand Tamerlane	25	2 50
127 ‡—— cheval noir	1 50	12
128 ‡—— Turk	50	4 50
129 ‡Imperatrice Romaine	1 50	12
130 King George	62	6
131 Prince Mauritz	25	2
132 ‡Queen of the Moors	50	5
133 Roi de Brasil	50	6
134 Roi de Congo	75	4
135 Triumph d'Amsterdam	25	2
136 Triumph d'Lille, *rectifié*	50	4 50
137 Violet King	50	4 50
138 —— Dorothé	75	6
139 ‡—— ma favorite	75	6
140 —— Prince de Galitz	75	6
141 ‡Washington, *singular*	1	8
30 finest varieties *by name*		3
20 fine do. *by name*		2
50 fine do. *mixed*	20	1 50

Red, rosy, crimson, and scarlet, on white grounds.

142 Absalom	37	3 50
143 ‡Agrandeur	50	4 50
144 ‡Bacu rectifié, *extra*	1 50	12
145 ‡Belle berdine	25	2
146 Cerise superbe, *extra*	3 25	30
147 ‡Cramoisie velonia	37	3
148 ‡Danae	50	4
149 Duke of Lancaster	37	3
150 Eleonora	25	2
151 ‡Globe terreste	25	2
152 Koningshof	25	2
153 La beauté fine	25	2
154 ‡La comtesse	75	6
155 La miniature	25	2

	Each. $ cts	Dozen. $ cts
156 La ravisante, *striped leaved*	25	2 50
157 Princess d'Asturie	50	4
158 Queen of England	75	6
159 ‡Reine des cerises	1	9
160 ‡—— de France	25	2 50
161 ‡Rose blandina, *extra*	50	4
162 ‡—— camusa	1 50	12
163 —— camusa de Craix, *extra*	2 50	20
164 —— clelie	50	4
165 ‡—— brilliante	1	9
166 —— la belle Helene	25	2
167 —— la Dauphine	37	3
168 —— Hebee	75	6
169 ‡—— tertia	1	9
170 ‡—— precieuse, *rectifié*	75	6
171 Soomerschoon	25	2
172 White crown, *bontlof, silver striped*	37	3
40 finest varieties *by name*		3
20 fine do. *by name*		2
50 fine do. *mixed*	20	1 50

Double Tulips.

	Each. $ cts	Dozen. $ cts
173 Admiral Kingsbergen	50	4
174 Barbarossa	50	4
175 Blanc bordre rouge	25	2
176 —— —— bleu, *producing often several flowers on one stalk*	25	2
177 Bizar canelle	25	2
178 ‡Buonaparte, *very large*	50	4 50
179 Caffé brun	25	2
180 ‡——— *flamed*	25	2 50
181 Concordia	25	2
182 Couleur de feu	25	2
183 Cour de Versailles	25	2
184 ‡Couronne d'Hollande	25	2
185 ‡——— imperiale	50	4 50
186 ‡——— d'or, *yellow flamed*	50	4 50
187 ——— blanche	31	3
188 Crenaad Conde	25	2
189 Duke Van Utrecht	25	2
190 —— Van Thol, *very early*	25	2

	Each. $ cts	Dozen. $ cts
191 Feathered, *or parrot*	37	3 50
192 Fisonimus	31	3
193 Gaillarda	50	4
194 Golden pæony	25	2
195 Grisdelin aimable	25	2
196 Groener ridder	25	2
197 Imperible	25	2
198 —— panaché	25	2 50
199 Jaune imperiale	50	4
200 ‡La sublime	50	4 50
201 Lion d'Hollande	25	2
202 ‡Marriage de ma fille, *extra*	50	4
203 ‡Mode d'Hollande	50	4 50
204 Olive brown	25	2 50
205 ‡Ophir	50	4
206 Orange crown	25	2
207 Orange throne	25	2
208 Pallas	25	2
209 Pæony red	25	2
210 Poolche roos	25	2
211 Pourpré imperiale	50	4
212 Prince Charles	25	2
213 ‡Proserpine	75	6
214 Rose printems	25	2
215 —— eclatante	25	2
216 ‡—— blanche	25	2
217 Rosa mundi	25	2
218 Rouge formidable	1	9
219 Salamander	50	4
220 —— *panaché*	75	6
221 Superville	25	2
222 ‡Tournesol, *extra, and very early*	1 50	15
223 Warande	25	2
224 ‡Yellow rose, *very fragrant*	25	2
225 Zenophon	50	4
60 finest varieties *by name*		2
75 fine do. *mixed*	20	1 50

| | Each. | Dozen. |
| | $ cts | $ cts |

Parrot Tulips.

*The leaves of these have feathered edges, and, in
addition to other colours, combine shades of green,
which no other Tulips do—from these circum-
stances their appearance is altogether unique.*

	Each.	Dozen.
226 Chevalier vert	25	2 50
227 Constantinople	25	2
228 Couleur de café	50	4 50
229 ‡Margrave of Baden, *extra*	37	3 50
230 ‡Perfecta, *extra*	37	3
231 Rubra major	50	4
232 ——— minor	25	2
233 Striped	37	3
234 Yellow major	31	3
235 ——— minor	25	2
finest varieties *by name*		2
fine do. *mixed*		1 50

Primo Baguet Tulips.

*These have very strong stems, and large fine shaped
cups.*

	Each.	Dozen.
236 Admiral general	75	6
237 Altesse royale	37	4
238 Amphion	75	6
239 Castor	50	4
240 Jupiter	50	5
241 Penelope	75	6
242 Thales	75	6
20 finest varieties *by name*		3
30 fine do. *mixed*		2

Grand Baguet Rigaut Tulips.

*These have exceedingly tall and strong stems, and
very large fine shaped cups.*

	Each.	Dozen.
243 Admiral	37	3
244 King David	50	4
245 Lycurgus	75	6
246 Merveille du monde	50	4

	Each.	Dozen.
	$ cts	$ cts
247 Pompe celebre	75	6
248 Samson	25	2
20 finest varieties *by name*		3
30 fine do. *mixed*		2

Breeder Tulips.

These, from possessing superior standard qualities, are selected by the Dutch as most suitable to break into new varieties.

	Each.	Dozen.
249 Bruno	25	2
250 Cerise primo	37	3
251 Couronne jaune	35	2
252 La comprice	25	2
253 Marons	25	2
254 Ponceau à la fin pourpre	25	2
255 Sang de bœuf	50	4
256 Violet decise	37	3
257 —— boe	25	2
258 —— lustre	50	4
259 —— rougeatre	25	2
30 finest varieties *by name*		2
40 fine do. *mixed*		1 50

TULIPS—*Distinct Species.*

		Each.	Dozen.
260 Cape	Tulipa breyniana	1	9
261 Sweet yellow Florentine	—— sylvestris	25	2
262 Clusius' Sicilian	—— Clusiana	1	9
263 Celsian Levant	—— Celsiana	1	9

TULIPS—*By Assortments.*

The first assortment of 100 Tulips, *of 100 exquisite varieties, one of each by name* $30

The second assortment of 100 do, *of 50 fine varieties, two of each by name*   20

The third assortment of 100 do. *of 25 good varieties, four of each by name*   18

The fourth assortment of 100 do. *of 20 varieties, five of each by name*   15

Various colours mixed, *per 100 roots*   12

Common mixed, *per 100 roots*   6

	Each.	Dozen.
	$ cts	$ cts

CROWN IMPERIALS.
Fritillaria *imperialis*.
Class, *Hexandria.* Order, *Monogynia.*

1 Chinese	25	2 50
2 Chapeau de Prince, *scarlet*	25	2 50
3 Crown on crown	37	3
4 ——————— *yellow*	37	3
5 Gelvia	37	3
6 Grand Alexander	75	6
7 Maximus, *large red*	37	3 50
8 Orange red	25	2 50
9 Pileus cardinalis, *crimson*	31	3
10 Prince hood, *scarlet*	25	2 50
11 Roman king, *red*	37	3
12 Royal standard	25	2 50
13 Rubro sulpherino	25	2 50
14 Sang de bœuf, *blood coloured*	25	2 50
15 Slagzwaard, *red*	25	2 50
16 William rex, *fine red*	25	2 50
17 Yellow	25	2 50
18 Double yellow	50	4 50
19 ———— red	50	4 50
20 ‡Gold striped	50	4 50
21 ‡Silver striped	50	4 50
30 varieties *by name*		2 50
Reds, *various kinds, mixed*	25	2 25
Yellows do. do.	25	2 25
Reds and yellows, *various kinds, mixed*	25	2 25

——

FRITILLARIES.
Class, *Hexandria.* Order, *Monogynia.*

1 Fritillaria persica, Persian Fritillary	25	2 25
2 ———— lanceolata, Missouri do.	1	10
3 ———— meleagris, chequered do.	25	2 50
4 ———— *Aigle noir*, black do.	25	2 50
5 ———— *Lucianus*, brown flamed do.	25	2 50
6 ———— *Pax alba*, white do.	25	2 50

	Each.	Dozen.
	$ cts	$ cts
7 Fritillaria, *Favorite*, yellow do.	25	2 50
8 ———————— *Surpassante*, do. spotted do.	25	2 50
9 ———————— *Cicero*, purple flamed	25	2 50
20 fine varieties *by name*		2 50
50 fine do. *mixed*	25	2

———

LILIES.

Class, *Hexandria*.   Order, *Monogynia*.

		Each	Dozen
1 Common white	Lilium candidum	12	1
2 ‡Double do.	—— *v. pleno*	37	3 25
3 ‡Striped leaved do. *superb*	—— *v. variegato* 1	25	12
4 Purple blotched do.	—— *v. maculato*	50	4 50
5 ‡Chinese tyger, *or leopard*	—— tygrinum	25	2
6 Bulb bearing	—— bulbiferum	25	1 50
7 Orange	—— *v. aurantium*	25	1 50
8 ‡Elegant silver striped	—— *v. varieg.* 2	50	25
9 ‡Superb	—— superbum	25	1 50
10 Canada	—— canadense	25	1 50
11 Philadelphia	—— philadelphicum	25	1 50
12 Catesby's	—— catesbæi	50	5
13 ‡Scarlet pompone	—— pomponium	37	3
14 ‡Yellow do.	—— *v. luteo*	37	3
15 Kamskatka	—— Kamskatense	25	2
16 ‡Scarlet chalcedonian	—— chalcedonicum	31	2 50
17 Chinese red	—— concolor	2	
18 Japan white	—— japonicum	5	

Martagon, or Turk's Cap Lilies.

Scarlet.

	Each	Dozen
19 Arcole	35	2 25
20 Caligula	31	2 50
21 Constantinople	31	2 50
22 Groot meester	31	3
23 Groot voorst	25	2 25
24 Romulus	25	2 25
25 Rubro Cæsar	31	2 50

H

	Each.	Dozen.
	$ cts	$ cts

Purple.

	Each $ cts	Dozen $ cts
26 Double violet flamed	50	4 50
27 Habit pourpre	25	2 25
28 Crown of Tunis	25	2 50
29 Pourpre fameuse	37	3
30 Purple brilliant	25	2 25

White.

31 Blanchart	25	2 25
32 Crown of Algiers	37	3
33 Crown of Jerusalem	37	3
34 Madame	25	2 50
35 Pure blanche	50	4

Yellow.

36 Good rose	25	2 25
37 Grand duke	31	2 50
38 Hero	25	2 25
39 Jaune hautesse	31	3
40 La trophée	37	3

Orange.

41 Hercules	25	2 25
42 King of Prussia	25	2 50
43 La Parisienne	37	3
60 fine varieties *by name*		2 25
75 do. *mixed*	25	2

—

AMARYLLIS.

Class, *Hexandria.*   Order, *Monogynia.*

		Each $ cts	Dozen $ cts
1 *‡Jacobean lily; *splendid*	Amaryllis formossissima	37	2 50
2 *‡Guernsey	———— sarniensis	50	4 50
3 *Wave flowered	———— undulata	25	2
4 Changeable, *from* *white to red*	———— atamasco	25	2
5 Yellow flowering	———— lutea	25	1 50
6 *‡White long leaved Cape	———— longifolia	1 50	12
7 *‡Rose coloured do.	———— *v. roseo*	1 50	12

		Each.$ cts	Dozen $ cts
8 *‡Superb riband striped Amaryllis *vittata*		2	20
9 *‡Belladona major ———— *belladona*		75	7 50
10 *———— media ———— *v. media*		75	7 50
11 *———— minor ———— *v. minor*		75	7 50
12 *———— one flowering ———— *v. uniflore*		75	7 50
13 *‡Barbadoes ———— *equestris, Brazilliensis, B. R.*		2	
14 *‡Double flowering do. ———— *v. pleno*		3	
15 *‡Mexican ———— *reginæ*		1 50	
16 *Saffron coloured ———— *crocata*		4	
17 *Curled flowered ———— *crispa - Strumaria, B. M.*		1	
18 *‡Chinese golden ———— *aurea*		3	
19 *‡Cape rose coloured ———— *capensis*		2	
20 *‡Yucca flowered, *or* Cape coast ———— *ornata spectabilis, B. R.*		8	
21 *Purple Cape ———— *purpurea*		2	
22 *Winged ———— *alata*		2	
23 *‡Striped flowering ———— *Johnsonii*		4	
24 *‡Fothergills curve leaved ———— *curviflora*		5	
25 *‡Snowdrop leaved ———— *radiata*		3	
26 *‡Net flowered ———— *reticulata*		4	
27 *‡Sickle leaved ———— *falcata Brunsvigia, B. M.*		8	
28 *‡Gigantic, *very splendid* ———— *gigantea*		30	
29 *‡Oriental ———— *orientalis*		12	

——

POLEANTHUS NARCISSUS.
Narcissus *tazetta*.
Class, *Hexandria*.. Order, *Monogynia*.

White, with Orange and Citron Cups.

1 Bazelman major		37
2 Czar of Moscow		25
3 Duke d'Ahremberg		31
4 Gloria mundi, *singular*		37

	Each.	Dozen.
	$ cts	$ cts
5 Grand monarque	50	
6 Jupiter	31	
7 Juno	31	
8 Luna	25	
9 Madame royale	25	
10 Medio luteo	31	
11 Monument	31	
12 Primo citroniere	25	
40 varieties *by name*		2 50
50 do. *mixed*		2

Yellow and Citron, with gold yellow Cups.

	Each.	Dozen.
13 Anselma	37	
14 Etoile d'or	37	
15 Gloria mundi	25	
16 Grand soleil d'or	25	
17 La mignonne	37	
18 Madouce	37	
19 Marianne	31	
20 Memorable	50	
21 Mylord	31	
22 Triumph	37	
40 varieties *by name*		2 50
50 do. *mixed*		2
White and yellow, *various kinds mixed*		2

Poleanthus Narcissus, *with double cups.*

	Each.	Dozen.
23 Belle Catharine	37	3
24 Belle bonne	37	3
25 Italian	25	2 50
26 La monstreuse	37	3
27 La triomphante	37	3
28 Lycurgus	25	2 50
29 Noblissimo	37	3

Double Narcissus, *or Daffodil.*

	Each.	Dozen.
30 Albo pleno odorato, *or white fragrant*	12	75
31 Incomparable	12	1
32 Orange Phœnix	12	75

	Each.	Dozen.
	$ cts	$ cts
33 Sulpher crown	12	1
34 Tratus cantus, *or hundred leaved*	12	1
35 Van Zion	12	1
Different varieties *mixed*		75

Single Narcissus.

	Each.	Dozen.
36 Albo odorato, *or white fragrant*	12	1
37 Biflorus	12	1
38 Bifrons	25	2
39 Bulbocodium, *or hoop petticoat*	25	2
40 Maximus	25	1
41 Moschatus	25	2
42 Nana minor	12	1
43 Nana major	12	1
44 Poeticus	12	1
45 Sulpher trumpet	12	1
46 Triandrus, *or reflexed*	25	2
47 Trumpet marin	12	1
48 ———— major	12	1
Different varieties *mixed*		1

Jonquils.

	Each.	Dozen.
49 Double fragrant	18	1 50
50 Large single	12	1
51 Single campernelle	12	1
52 Small fragrant	12	1
Different varieties *mixed*		1

RANUNCULUS *Asiaticus, or Crowfoot.*
Class, *Polyandria.* Order, *Polygynia.*

Double Persian.

	Each.	Dozen.
1 Rose coloured, *mixed varieties*	20	1 50
2 Olive do. do.	20	1 50
3 Orange do. do.	20	1 50
4 Bright crimson do.	20	1 50
5 Bright red and pink do.	20	1 50
6 Yellow do.	20	1 50

		Each. $ cts	Dozen, $ cts
7	Yellow striped, *mixed varieties*	20	1 50
8	White, and white spotted, do.	20	1 50
9	White striped, do.	20	1 50
10	Dark brown and coffee coloured, do.	20	1 50
11	Black and purple, do.	20	1 50
12	Violet, do.	20	1 50
	Finest varieties, *mixed all colours*		1 50
	Ditto do. *per* 100 $ 4 *to* $ 6		

Different Species.

		Each. $ cts	Dozen, $ cts
13	Scarlet turban	12	1 50
14	Constantinople, *or Turkey*	20	1 50
15	Seraphique d'Algiers	20	1 50
16	Roman	20	1 50
17	Marvellous	25	1 50
18	Rutæfolius, *or rue leaved*	25	2

ANEMONE *Coronaria, or Wind Flower*
Class, *Polyandria.* Order, *Polygynia.*

		Each. $ cts	Dozen, $ cts
1	Double rosy and crimson, *mixed varieties*	20	1 50
2	——— red and pink do.	20	1 50
3	——— dark blue do.	20	1 50
4	——— white, and white spotted, do.	20	1 50
	Finest varieties, *mixed all colours*		1 50
	Ditto do. *per* 100 $ 4 *to* $ 6		

Different Species.

		Each. $ cts	Dozen, $ cts
5	Anemone hortensis, *single red*	20	2
6	——— ——— *double red*	25	2 50
7	——— ——— *purple*	20	2
8	——— ——— *pale purple*	20	2
9	——— ——— *violet*	20	2
10	——— ——— *scarlet*	25	2 50
11	——— ——— *flame coloured*	25	2 50
12	——— appenina	25	2 50
13	——— thalictroides	12	75
14	——— ——— double	50	5

	Each.	Dozen.
	$ cts	$ cts
15 Anemone nemorosa, *purpureo*	20	1 50
16 ———— ———— *purpureo pleno*	25	2
17 ———— ———— *albo pleno*	25	2
18 ——— pulsatilla, *ceruleo*	25	2
19 ——— sylvestris, *albo pleno*	25	2
20 ——— hepatica	12	1
21 ——— ———— *pleno*	50	5
22 ——— pensylvanica	25	2
23 ——— virginica	25	2

IRIS, *or Flower de Luce.*
Class, *Triandria.* Order, *Monogynia.*
Spanish Bulbous Iris.

1 Blue feuillemort
2 Cornelia
3 Imperial porcelain
4 Jaune constant
5 Louis d'or
6 La plaisante
7 Magazin des couleurs
8 Minerva
9 Morleon
10 Pallido

30 varieties *by name*	25	2
Different varieties *mixed*	12	1 25
Double flowering Spanish Iris	1	9

English Bulbous Iris.

11 Alcibiades
12 Duke of Tuscany
13 Hecuba
14 Incomparable purple
15 Imperatrice de France
16 Menelaus

20 varieties *by name*	21	2
Different varieties *mixed*	25	1 25

	Each.	Dozen.
	$ cts	$ cts

Iris Pavonia, or Peacock Iris.

17 *White	62	
18 *Blue	62	
19 *Pale blue	62	
20 *Purple	62	
21 *Violet	62	

Different Species.

22 Iris susiana, or Chalcedonian	50	4
23 —— tuberosa, or Snake's head	37	
24 *— longifolia	50	
25 Persian	12	1

Fibrous Iris, *many species, see page 57.*

CROCUS.

Class, *Triandria.* Order, *Monogynia.*

1 Belle mignonne		
2 Brown violet		
3 Cloth of gold		
4 Eleonora		
5 Gold yellow		
6 Large white		
7 —— yellow		
8 —— blue		
9 Dark purple		
10 Morleon		
11 Pale purple		
12 Purple variegated		
13 Saffron, *autumn flowering*		
14 Scotch		
30 varieties *by name*	8	75
Spring flowering, *different varieties mixed*		50
Autumn flowering		75

	Each.	Dozen.
	$ cts	$ cts

COLCHICUM *Autumnale,* or *Meadow Saffron.*
Class, *Hexandria.* Order, *Trigynia.*

1 White
2 Agathe variegated
3 Violet
4 Violet variegated
5 Byzantea major
6 Striped leaved
7 Double white
8 ———— agathe flamed
9 ———— agathe variegated
10 Spring flowering, *or Bulbocodium vernum*

	Each	Dozen
All the above varieties *by name*	25	2
Autumn flowering *mixed*	20	1 50
Spring flowering *mixed*	20	1 50

*IXIAS.
Class, *Triandria.* Order, *Monogynia.*

1 Ixia bicolor
2 —— conica
3 ——————— *sulphureo intus nigro*
4 —— crocata, *major*
5 —— ———— *hyalina aurea*
6 —— ———— *liliacea rubro*
7 —— corymbosa, *purpurea*
8 —— longiflora
9 —— maculata, *viridi*
10 —— palmæfolia
11 —— polystachya
12 —— ———————— *ceruleo maculato*
13 —— pratensis, *coccinea*
14 —— ———————— *luteo intus nigro*
15 —— stellata
16 —— tricolor
17 —— tubiflora
18 —— brilliante, *ceruleo*

	Each	Dozen
60 varieties *by name*	50	4

	Each. $ cts	Dozen. $ cts

GLADIOLUS, *Corn Flag, or Sword Lily.*

Class, *Triandria.* Order, *Monogynia.*

1 Gladiolus communis, *purple*	12	1
2 ———— ———— *rose coloured*	20	1 50
3 ———— ———— *large red*	12	1
4 ———— ———— *flesh coloured*	20	1 50
5 ———— ———— *white*	20	1 50
6 ———— byzantinus, *or Turkish flag*	25	2
7 ———— cardinalis, *or large scarlet*	50	3 50
8 ———— ———— *albo*	50	4
9 *———— undulatus, *or wave flowered*	50	4
10 *———— watsonius, *or scarlet flag*	1	
11 *———— *tyger yellow*	1	
12 *———— *large African*	1	
13 *———— *large American*	1	

ERYTHRONIUM DENS CANIS, *or Dog's Tooth Violet.*

Class, *Hexandria.* Order, *Monogynia.*

1 Purple	18	1 50
2 Red	18	1 50
3 White	18	1 50
4 Blotched leaved	12	1

ORNITHOGALUM, *or Star of Bethlehem.*

Class, *Hexandria.* Order, *Monogynia.*

1 Pyramidal, or Neapolitan Ornithogalum pyramidale	37	3
2 Blue do. ——— *v. ceruleum*	50	4
3 White umbelled ——— *umbellatum*	10	75

U   Golden do. do.

9 *White Arabian	—— arabicum	1	
10 *Yellow do.	—— v. aureo	2	
11 *White African	—— africanum	1	

——◆——

SCILLA, *or Squill.*
Class, *Hexandria.*   Order, *Monogynia.*

1 Starry squill, *or Peru- vian hyacinth* }	Scilla peruviana	50	4
2 Blue do.	—— v. cerulea	50	4
3 Siberian	—— siberica	25	2 50
4 Nodding	—— amœna	25	2 50
5 Bell shaped	—— campanulata	25	2
6 Two leaved, *white flowering* }	—— bifolia	50	5
7 ——— *blue do.*	—— v. ceruleo	50	5
8 *Hyacinth flowered.	—— hyacinthoides	37	3
9 *Officinal	—— maritima	1	

——◆——

ALLIUM, *or Garlick.*
Class, *Hexandria.*   Order, *Monogynia.*

1 Homer's moly	Allium nigrum	25	2
2 Purple flowering do.	—— v. purpureo	25	2
3 Large yellow flowering	—— moly	25	1 50
4 —— white do.	—— v. albo	25	1 50
5 —— red do.	—— v. roseo	25	2
6 Striped leaved	—— v. fol. var.	25	2
7 Three seeded	—— tricoccum	20	1 50
8 Swiss purple headed	—— descendens	50	6

CHOICE BULBOUS AND FIBROUS ROOTS.

			Each. $ cts	Dozen. $ cts
1	Purple dragon	Arum dracunculus	1	9
2	Green do.	—— dracontium	1	9
3	Painted arum	—— triphyllum	12	1 25
4	Lance leaved claytonia	Claytonia lanceolata	20	1 50
5	Solomon's seal, 4 *species*	Convallaria, 4 *species*	12	75
6	Siberian fumitory	Fumaria bulbosa	25	2 50
7	English snowdrop	Galanthus nivalis	12	1
8	Double do.	—————— *v. pleno*	12	1
9	Tuberous rooted glycine	Glycine apios	12	1
10	Yellow winter aconite	Helleborus hyemalis	25	2
11	Yellow plumed helonias	Helonias dioica	25	2
12	Spring snowflake	Leucojum vernum	20	1 50
13	Double snowflake	———— *v. pleno*	50	5
14	Summer do.	———— æstivum	20	1 50
15	Blue blazing star	Liatris scariosa	25	1 50
16	Spiked liatris	—— spicata	25	1 50
17	Hairy do.	—— pilosa	25	1 50
18	Tuberous limodorum	Limodorum tuberosum	20	1 50
19	*Single tuberose	Polyanthes tuberosa	12	1
20	*Double do.	———— *v. pleno*	12	1
21	*Striped leaved do.	———— *v. fol. var.*	50	5
22	White ivy leaf	Prenanthes alba	20	1 50
23	Virginian lungwort	Pulmonaria virginica	25	2 50
24	Indian puccoon, *or* } blood root	Sanguinaria canadensis	12	1
25	Trillium, 3 *species*	Trillium, 3 *species*	25	2
26	Perfoliate uvularia	Uvularia perfoliata	12	75
27	Sessile leaved do.	—— sessilifolia	12	75

N. B. For other choice Bulbs, see Green-House Plants.

GREEN-HOUSE TREES, SHRUBS, AND PLANTS.

All of which will thrive in a comfortable sitting-room during the winter—they are in either pots or boxes, and the prices are inclusive. Those which have no prices attached to them will not be for sale until the autumn of 1824.

N. B. Those checked thus * though generally cultivated as Green-House Plants, will stand the winters of the middle States in the open air.

1 Prickly leaved acacia	Acacia armata	$1	
2 African blue lily	Agapanthus umbellatus	1	50
3 Pale do. do.	———— v. pallido	2	
4 American century Aloe	Agave americana		75
5 Striped leaved do.	—— v. folio striato	1	
6 *Virginian do.	—— virginica		75
7 Tallest albuca	Albuca altissima	1	
8 Great do.	—— major	1	
9 Small do.	—— minor	1	
10 Green flowered aletris	Aletris capensis	3	
11 Soccotrine aloe	Aloe soccotrina	1	
12 Partridge breast do.	—— variegata	1	
13 Cushion do.	—— retusa		75
14 Trifoliate do.	—— trifoliata	1	
15 Tongue do.	—— lingua		75
16 Pearl tongue do.	—— margaritifera		75
17 Cobweb do.	—— arachnoides	1	
18 Two coloured do.	—— discolor	1	
19 Attenuated do.	—— attenuata	1	
20 Warted do.	—— verrucosa	1	
21 Spotted leaved do.	—— maculata, &c.	1	
22 Peruvian spotted alstroemeria	Alstroemeria pelegrina	1	50
23 Striped flowered do.	—— ligtu	2	
24 Rock alyssum of Crete	Alyssum saxatile		75
25 Amaryllis, *a splendid assortment, see page 86*	Amaryllis, *see page 86*		
26 Ginger	Amomum zingiber	1	
27 Fetid bean trefoil	Anagyris foetida		
28 *Andromeda, *or sorrel tree*	Andromeda arborea	1	
29 *Anemone, *see page 90*	Anemone		

I

30 Ethiopean antholyza	Antholyza ethiopica	$1
31 Tube flowered do.	—————— tubulosa	1
32 Scarlet do.	————— cardinalis	1
33 Narrow leaved do.	————— angustifolia	1
34 Orange coloured do.	————— aurantiaca	1
35 Great orange do.	————— v. major	1
36 Minor rose coloured do.	————— minor, roseo	1
37 ——— red do.	————— v. rubro	1
38 Jupiter's beard	Anthyllis barba-jovis	1
39 Hermannia leaved do.	————— hermannia	1
40 European strawberry tree	Arbutus unedo	1
41 Double flowering do.	————— v. pleno	2
42 Great flowering arctotis	Arctotis superba	1
43 Chinese ardisia	Ardisia crenata	2
44 Chili shining aristotelia	Aristotelia macqui	3
45 Silvery leaved wormwood	Artemesia argentea	1
46 Chinese do.	————— sinensis	1
47 Striped European reed	Arundo donax, fol. var.	2
48 African swallowwort	Asclepias fruticosa	1
49 Curassavian superb do.	————— curassavica	1
50 Cape atragene	Atragene capensis	3
51 Purslane tree	Atriplex halimus	1
52 Japan-gold dust tree	Aucuba japonica	1
53 Chinese azalea	Azalea indica	5
54 Serrated Banksia, and other species	Banksia serrata, &c.	
55 Chinese bæckia	Bæckia frutescens	
56 Chinese two coloured begonia	Begonia evansiana	1
57 *Daisy, see page 59	Bellis	
58 *Lewis's mountain holly	Berberis aquifolium	2
59 Chinese barberry	————— sinensis	
60 Norfolk Island trumpet flower	Bignonia pandora	2
61 *Chinese great do.	————— grandiflora	1
62 *Four winged do.	————— capreolata	75
63 Upright do.	————— stans	2
64 Heart leaved anatto	Bixa orellana	2
65 Chinese bocconia	Bocconia cordata	2
66 Privet leaved borya	Borya ligustrina	1
67 Pointed do. do.	————— acuminata	1
68 Mexican scarlet bouvardia, or Houstonia	Bouvardia triphylla	2
69 American brunfelsia	Brunfelsia americana	
70 Rush leaved Buonapartia	Buonapartia juncea	

71 Yellow flowering buphthalmum	Buphthalmum frutescens	$ 1
72 Chili globe flower	Buddlea globosa	1
73 Shrubby hare's ear	Bupleurum fruticosum	1
74 Minorca box tree	Buxus balearicus	75
75 Creeping cereus	Cactus flagelliformis	1
76 Great night blooming do.	——— grandiflorus	2
77 Melon thistle	——— mammillaris	75
78 Wave torch thistle	——— repandus	1
79 Yellow spined Indian fig	——— tuna	1
80 Purple flowered do.	——— speciosus	1
81 Cochineal do.	——— cochenillifer, &c.	1
82 Brazilletto wood	Cæsalpina paniculata	2
83 Two coloured arum	Caladium bicolor	2
84 Ethiopian fragrant lily	Calla ethiopica	1
85 Hoary Malabar callicarpa	Callicarpa cana	2
86 Bermuda mulberry	——— americana	1
87 Chinese calycanthus	Calycanthus præcox	1
88 Single red camellia, or Japan rose	Camellia japonica	2
89 Semidouble red do.	——— *semipleno*	5
90 Double red do.	——— *rubro pleno*	5
91 Single white fragrant do.	——— *albo simplici*	10
92 Double white do.	——— *albo pleno*	5
93 Double pink, or *middlemist* do.	——— *carneo. pl.*	5
94 Double striped do.	——— *variegata*	5
95 Double crimson do.	——— *atrorubens*	$5 to 8
96 Anemone flowered, or *purple warrata* do.	——— *anemonæflora*	5 to 8
97 *Pompone, *white warrata*, or *white anemone* do.	——— *mutabilis*	8 to 10
98 Pæony flowered do.	——— *pæonæflora*	8 to 10
99 Double buff, or *maiden's blush* do.	——— *flavescens*	6 to 8
100 Fragrant myrtle leaved do.	——— *myrtifolia*	6 to 10
101 Blotched leaved do.	——— *maculata*	10
102 Lady Banks's tea leaved do.	——— *sasanqua*	8 to 10
103 Double flowering do.	do.——— *v. pleno*	
104 Red branched	do.——— *rubricaulis*	
105 Axillary flowered	do.——— *axillaris*	
106 Starry flowered	do.——— hexangulare	
107 Welbankian	do.——— Welbankii	

108 *Pyramidal bell flower   Campanula pyramidalis $ 1
109 Canary bell flower   Canarina campanula
110 Scarlet flowering Indian shot   Canna indica   75
111 Yellow flowering do.   —— flaccida   1
112 Superb cantua   Cantua coronopifolia   1
113 Caper tree   Capparis spinosa   3
114 Bird pepper   Capsicum baccatum   1
115 Corymbose flowering cassia   Cassia corymbosa   2
116 Downy leaved do.   —— tomentosa   2
117 Hottentot cherry   Cassine maurocenia   3
118 Chinese nettle tree   Celtis sinensis   3
119 Cape centaury   Centaurea capensis   1
120 St. John's bread   Ceratonia siliqua   5
121 Day smelling cestrum   Cestrum diurnum   1
122 Night smelling do.   —— nocturnum   1
123 Chili willow leaved do.   —— parqui
124 Cabbage palm   Chamærops palmetto   1
125 Woolly chaptalia   Chaptalia tomentosa   1
126 *Wallflower   Cheiranthus cheiri   50
127 Double bloody do.   —— v. pleno   1
128 Semidouble do.   —— v. semipleno   1
129 Stock gillyflower, many varieties   —— incanus, 50 cts. to $1
130 Chili bearded chelone   Chelone barbata   1
131 Madeira chrysanthemum   Chrysanthemum pinnatifidum   1
132 *Chinese do. for eleven splendid varieties see page 56.   —— indicum
133 Shrubby golden locks   Chrysocoma coma-aurea   1
134 Purple canary aster   Cineraria lanata   75
135 Silvery leaved ragwort   —— maritima   1
136 Cretan cistus   Cistus creticus   1
137 White leaved do. &c.   —— albidus, &c.   1
138 Seville orange   Citrus aurantium
139 Double flowering do.   —— flore pleno
140 Hermaphrodite do.   —— var.
141 Distorted do.   —— var.
142 Gold striped do.   —— aureo variegato
143 Silver striped do.   —— argenteo variegato
144 Silver striped curled leaved do.   —— argen. var. crispa

145 Silver striped willow leaved orange	} Citrus, *salicifolia var.*	$5
146 Myrtle leaved do.	------ *myrtifolia*	
147 Bergamot do.	------ *aromatica*	
148 St. Salvador sweet do.	------ *pyriformis*	
149 Red cored Malta sweet do.	------ *sanguineus*	
150 China sweet do.	------ sinensis	
151 ------ curled leaved do.	------ *humile*	
152 ------ mandarin do.	------ nobilis	5
153 ------ cherry size do.	------ *minor*	
154 Tangiers do.	------ tanjierano	5
155 Three leaved do.	------ trifoliata	
156 Turkish do.	------ *lunata*	
157 Violet begarade do.	------ *violacea*	
158 Horned begarade do.	------ *cornuta*	
159 Forbidden fruit do.	------ *Adami*	
160 Shaddock, *monstrous fruit*	------ decumana	
161 Lisbon lemon	------ limon	
162 Imperial do.	------ *var.*	
163 Pear shaped do.	------ *pyriformis*	
164 Red fruited lemon of Ponsino	} ------ *sanguineus*	
165 Gold striped do.	------ *aureo striato*	5
166 Monstrous lemon	------ *v. tuberosa*	
167 Madeira citron	------ medica	
168 Palermo solid do.	------ *var.*	
169 Cedra do.	------ *cedra*	
170 West-India lime	------ limonella	

Orange, Lemon, Citron, Shaddock, and Lime **Trees,**
  one year inoculated, (except those noted)   2 50
Ditto *two years do.*   3
Ditto *three years do in a bearing state*   3 50

171 Great Japan virgin's bower	Clematis florida	1
172 Double flowering do.	------ *v. pleno*	2
173 Sweet scented do.	------ flammula	1
174 Evergreen do.	------ cirrhosa	1
175 India clerodendrum	{ Clerodendrum sipho nanthus }	3
176 Madeira tree clethra	Clethra arborea	3
177 Widow wail	Cneorum tricoccum	1
178 Mexican climbing cobæa	Cobæa scandens	2
179 Coffee tree	Coffea arabica	2
180 Scarlet cape bladder senna	Colutea frutescens	1

181 Chinese convolvulus	Convolvulus, *sp* *from China*	$ 1
182 Chinese punctated cookia	Cookia punctata	
183 Japan globe flower	Corchorus japonicus	1
184 Yellow flowering coronilla	Coronilla glauca	1
185 White flowered correa	Correa alba	1
186 Round leaved cape na-velwort	Cotydelon orbiculata	1
187 Large calyxed do. *or air plant*	——— pinnata, *or Bryo-phyllum calycinum*	1
188 Chinese hawthorn	Cratægus glabra	2
189 Indian do.	———— indica	5
190 Acute leaved crassula	Crassula acutifolia	1
191 White flowering do.	——— lactea	1
192 Searlet do. do.	——— coccinea	1
193 American crinum	Crinum americanum	5
194 African do.	——— africanum	5
195 Asiatic do.	——— asiaticum	
196 Pubescent do.	——— pubescens	
197 Cretan evergreen cypress	Cupressus sempervirens	1
198 Sago palm	Cycas revoluta	3
199 Persian cyclamen	Cyclamen persicum	75
200 Round leaved spring do.	——— coum	1
201 *White autumnal do.	——— europæum	1
202 *Red do. do.	——— *v. roseo*	1
203 Ivy leaved do.	——— hederæfolium,&c.	1 50
204 Japan red flowering quince	Cydonia japonica	5
205 Narrow leaved cyrtanthus	Cyrtanthus angustifolius	
206 Oblique leaved do.	——— obliquus	
207 Japan cytisus	Cytisus japonicus	1
208 Cluster flowered do.	——— capitatus	1

Single Dahlias.

209 Dark purple dahlia	Dahlia superflua	75
210 Pale do do.	*v. pallida*	50
211 Dwarf do. do.	*v. nana*	50
212 Lilac coloured do.	*v. lilacina*	75
213 Velvet crimson do.	*v. atrorubro*	1
214 Brown do.	*v. fulva*	50
215 Dark red do.	*v. rubra*	50
216 Bright red do.	*v. fulgens*	75
217 Rose coloured do.	*v. rosea*	75
218 Yellow do.	*v. flava*	1

219 Orange coloured dahlia   Dahlia, *v. aurantia* $ 1
220 Scarlet   do.   *v. coccinea*   1
221 White   do.   *v. alba*   1

Double Dahlias.

222 Double orange dahlia	Dahlia *v. aurantia, pl.*	1
223 Superb do do	*v. aur. superba*	1 50
224 Buff do	*v. fulva*	1 50
225 Purple do	*v. speciosa*	1 50
226 Unrivalled purple do	*v. purp. splendens*	2
227 Favourite do do	*superba*	1 50
228 Dwarf lilac do	*humilis*	1 50
229 Nankin coloured do	*v. aurea*	1 50
230 Agathe do do	*v. pallida*	1 50
231 Rose do do	*v. rosea*	1 50
232 Superb rose do	*v. rosea superba*	2
233 White do	*v. alba*	1 50
234 White agathe do	*v. albida*	1 50
235 Red do	*v. rubra*	1 50
236 Favourite red do	*elegans*	1 50
237 Deep crimson do	*v. ardens*	2
238 Dwarf do do	*v. atrorubro*	1 50
239 Royal do do	*superba*	1 50
240 Elégant do do	*elegans*	1 50
241 Orange & flesh coloured do	*v. bicolor*	1 50
242 Yellow and do do	*superba*	1 50
243 Black do	*v. nigra*	2
244 Copper coloured do	*v. cuprœa*	1 50
245 Velvet do	*v. lilacina*	1 50
246 Sulpher coloured do	*v. ochroleuca*	1 50
247 Scarlet do	*v. coccinea*	2
248 Violet striped do	*v. pulchra striata*	2
249 Great flowered do	*v. grandiflora*	1 50
250 Fragrant Indian daphne	Daphne odora,	$ 1 to 2
251 Silver striped do	*v. argen. striato*	5
252 Trailing do	cneorum	1
253 Silver striped trailing do	*v. argen. striato*	3
254 Olive leaved do	oleæfolia	3
255 Evergreen spurge laurel	laureola	1
256 Flax leaved daphne	gnidium	3
257 Pontic twin flowered do	pontica, &c.	2
258 Neapolitan do	collina	2
259 Alpine do	alpina	2
260 Silvery leaved do	tartonraira	3

261 Great Peruvian datura	Dàtura arborea	$ 1
262 Creeping decumaria	Decumaria sarmentosa	1
263 Blue flowered-dianella	Dianella cerulea	1
264 *Carnation, see page 54.	Dianthus caryophyllus	
265 Syrian shrubby pink	fruticosus	2
266 Chinese rough fruited leechee	Dimocarpus litchi	
267 Chinese smooth fruited do	longan	
268 Yam	Dioscorea sativa	1
269 Venus's fly trap	Dionæa muscipula	75
270 Heath leaved diosma	Diosma alba	1
271 Japan date plum	Diospyros kaki	5
272 Canary dragon tree	Dracæna canariense	
273 Balm of Gilead	Dracocephalum canariense	75
274 Chinese oleaster	Eleagnus latifolius	5
275 Narrow leaved do	angustifolius	2
276 Carolina elytraria	Elytraria virgata	1
277 Chinese enkianthus	Enkianthus quinqueflora	
278 African heath	Erica mediterranea	1
279 Honeywort do	cerinthoides	2
280 Gray fine leaved do	cinerea	1
281 Sparrowwort do	passerina	1
282 Pubescent do	pubescens	1
283 Scotch red do. or heather	vulgaris	1
284 —— white do	v. albo	1
285 Double flowering do	v. pleno	2
286 Cross leaved heath	tetralix	1
287 White do do	v. albo	1
288 White Portugal hairy do	ciliaris	1
289 Purple do do	v. purpurea	1
290 Many flowering do	multiflora, or vagans	1
291 Red do do.	v. rubra	1
292 Dwarf early flowering do	herbacea	1
293 Verticillate flowered do	verticillata	2
294 Madeira tree do	arborea	1
295 Three flowered do	triflora	2
296 Arbutus flowered do	baccans	1
297 Black tipped do	nigritta	1
298 Coral plant	Erythrina herbacea	1
299 Coxcomb coral tree	crista galli	5
300 Gum eucalyptus, and other species	Eucalyptus robusta, &c.	
301 Blotched leaved eucomis	Eucomis punctata	1
302 Wave leaved do	undulata	1

303 Solitary flowered-eugenia Eugenia uniflora $ 2
304 Narrow leaved do   jambos   2
305 Japan burning bush   Euonymus japonicus
306 Sun spurge   Euphorbia helioscopia   1
307 Yellow naked flowered do   nudiflora   1
308 Japan ash leaved fagara   Fagara piperita
309 Mexican tyger flower   Feraria tygridia   50
310 Crisp flowered do   undulata   1
311 Branching do   antherosa
312 Chinese trailing fig   Ficus stipulata   1
313 Syrian fontanesia   Fontanesia phillyræoides 2
314 Scarlet f chsia, *or eardrop* Fuchsia coccinea   1
315 Single flowered cape jas- } Gardenia florida
   mine   }
316 Double small leaved do   *v. pleno*   2
317 Double broad leaved do   *v. major* $ 2 to 3
318 Dwarf small flowered do   radicans   2
319 Star flowered do   thunbergia   5
320 Verticillate flowered do   verticillata
321 Bushy do.   dumetorum   5
322 *Carolina yellow do   Gelseminum nitidum   1
324 Dyer's broom, &c.   Genista tinctoria   1
325 Italian tuberous geranium Geranium tuberosum   75
326 Sword-lily, *or corn flag* Gladiolus, *see page* 94.
327 Single seeded gleditschia Gleditschia monosperma 1
328 Chinese glycine   Glycine, *sp. from China* 2
329 Large flowering gloxinia Gloxinia speciosa
330 Flax leaved gnidia   Gnidia simplex
331 Pine leaved do   pinifolia
332 Loblolly bay   Gordonia lasianthus   1
333 Splendid flowering gorteria Gorteria rigens   1
334 Downy leaved grislea   Grislea tomentosa   2
335 Scarlet blood flower   Hæmanthus coccineus   3
336 White hæmanthus   albiflorus   4
337 Tyger do   tigrinus   4
338 Hairy do   ciliaris   12
339 Wave leaved do   puniceus
340 Hakea, *several species* Hakea, *sp.*
341 *Poetic, *or classic ivy* Hedera poetica   1
342 Garland flower   Hedychium coronarium   1
343 Peruvian heliotrope   Heliotropium peruvianum 1
344 Broad leaved do   parviflorum   1
345 Japan white day lily   Hemerocallis japonica   2
346 Twining hibbertia   Hiobertia volubilis   2

347 Chinese changeable hibiscus	Hibiscus mutabilis	$ 5
348 ——— rose do	rosa sinensis	3
349 ——— yellow do	v. flore luteo	
350 ——— double crimson do	v. rubro pl.	4
351 ——— maple leaved do	acerifolius	4
352 ——— palmated do	manihot	3
353 Purple flowered do	phœniceus	2
354 Great flowering do	grandiflorus	1
355 Scarlet flowering do	speciosus	1
356 Scabrous do	scaber	1
357 Sweet Japan hovenia	Hovenia dulcis	
358 Chinese splendid hoya	Hoya carnosa	3
359 *Chinese changeable hydrangea	Hydrangea hortensis	62
360 Chinese St. John's-wort	Hypericum monogynum	1
361 Star flowered hypoxis	Hypoxis stellata	2
362 Italian evergreen candytuft	Iberis sempervirens	1
363 Paraguay, or Yapan tea	Ilex vomitoria	1
364 Small leaved holly	cassine	1
365 Dahoon do	dahoon	1
366 Yellow flowered aniseed tree	Illicium parviflorum	1
367 Red do do	floridanum	
368 Botany-Bay indigo	Indigofera australis	2
369 Soldier wood of India	Inga purpurea	
370 Chinese fringed iris	Iris fimbriata	1
371 Silver striped do	v. folio varieg.	1
372 Peacock iris, see page 92.	pavonia	
373 Ixia, see page 93.	Ixia	
374 Chinese ixora	Ixora coccinea	
375 Catalonian jasmine	Jasminum grandiflorum	1
376 Silver striped do	officinale, arg. var.	1
377 Gold do do	v. aureo var.	
378 Lance leaved do	lanceolatum	
379 Yellow Indian do	odoratissimum	1
380 Azorian, or Madeira do	azoricum	1
381 Chinese curled flowered do	revolutum	1
382 Slender branched do	gracile	1
383 White Arabian do	sambac	1
384 Double do do	v. pleno	5
385 White Malabar nut	Justicia alhatoda	1
386 Blue flowered justicia	cerulea	1
387 Panicled do	paniculata	2

388 Peruvian justicia	Justicia peruviana	$ 2
389 Painted leaved do	picta	5
390 Dingy flowered Kennedia	Kennedia rubicunda	1 50
391 Scarlet do do	coccinea	2
392 *Chinese panicled koelreuteria	Koelreuteria paniculata	3
393 Pendulous flowered lachenalia	Lachenalia pendula	75
394 Tricoloured do	tricolor	75
395 Green flowered do	viridis	50
396 Yellow do. do	flava	1
397 Four coloured do	quadricolor	
398 Orchis do	orchioides	
399 Rose do do	rosea	
400 Purple do do	purpurea	1
401 Pink lagerstræmia, *superb*	Lagerstræmia indica	1
402 Purple do.	*v. purpurea*	1
403 Crimson do	*v. atrorubro*	1
404 New-Holland lambertia	Lambertia formosa	
405 Changeable lantana	Lantana camara	1
406 White do	alba	
407 European sweet bay	Laurus nobilis	75
408 Narrow leaved bay	*v. angustifolia*	1
409 Variegated leaved do	*v. fol. varieg.*	
410 Camphor tree	camphora	
411 Carolina do	caroliniensis	1
412 Fragrant lavendar	Lavandula dentata	50
413 Shrubby sea lavatera	Lavatera maritima	1
414 New-Zealand tea	Leptospermum scoparium	
415 Vanilla scented liatris	Liatris odoratissima	75
416 Wax tree of China	Ligustrum japonicum	5
417 Egyptian privet	*sp. nova*	2
418 Chinese limodorum	Limodorum tankervillæi	1 50
419 Trifoliate limonia	Limonia trifoliata	
420 Fulgent lobelia	Lobelia fulgens	1
421 Splendid do	splendens	1
422 Japan honeysuckle	Lonicera japonica	1
423 Dark flowered lotus	Lotus jacobæus	1
424 New-Holland do	australis	1
425 Erect do	erectus	75
426 Trailing do	corniculatus	75
427 Chinese coronet lychnis	Lychnis coronata	1
428 *Fulgent do	fulgens	2
429 Chinese lycium	Lycium sinense	

430 Mexican lythrum	Lythrum alatum	$1
431 Virgate do	virgatum	1
432 Chinese purple magnolia	Magnolia obovata	$2 to 3
433 chandelier do	conspicua	4 to 5
434 olive coloured do	fuscata	4 to 5
435 small flowered do	v. annonœfolia	5
436 dwarf do	pumila	2 to 3
437 slender branched do	tomentosa	8
438 Great laurel leaved do	grandiflora	1
439 Exmouth, or irony leav- ed do	v. ferruginea	2
440 Thick leaved malpighia	Malpighia crassifolia	
441 Italian tree medick	Medicago arborea	1
442 Heath leaved melaleuca	Melaleuca ericifolia	2
443 Hypericum leaved do	hypericifolia	2
444 Pale flowered do	armillaris	2
445 Whorl leaved do	densa	2
446 Pubescent do	pubescens	2
447 Myrtle leaved do	myrtifolia	
448 Splendid do	splendens	
449 Rush leaved cape melan- thium	Melanthium junceum	2
450 Great honey flower	Melianthus major	1
451 Smooth leaved fig mary- gold	Mesembryanthemum glabrum	50
452 Bearded do	barbatum	75
453 Splendid do	spectabile	1
454 Scimitar leaved do	acinaciforme	1
455 Two coloured do	bicolorum	1
456 Broad tongue do	linguæforme	1
457 Slender tongue do	angustum	75
458 Delta leaved do. &c.	deltoides	1
459 Japan broad leaved mes- pilus, or loquat	Mespilus japonica	3
460 Pinchaw of China	tomentosa	
461 Spear leaved metrosideros	Metrosideros lanceolata	2
462 Margined do	marginata	3
463 Laurel leaved do	laurifolia	
464 Vera Cruz sensitive tree	Mimosa pigra	2
465 Divaricated mimosa do	divaricata	1
466 Farnesian sweet do. or appoponax	farnesiana	1
467 Splendid monsonia	Monsonia speciosa	5
468 Sword leaved moræa	Moræa iridioides	1
469 Long flowered do	longiflora	1

470 Common Roman myrtle	Myrtus communis	$0	50
471 Rosemary leaved do	*rosmarinifolia*	2	
472 Orange leaved do	*boetica*	1	
473 Broad leaved Dutch do	*belgica*		75
474 Double flowering do	*v. pleno*	1	
475 Italian upright do	*italica*		75
476 Silver striped do do	*v. argen. varieg.*	1	
477 Gold striped do do	*v. aureo. varieg.*		
478 Portugal do	*lusitanica*	1	
479 Three leaved, *or Jew's do*	*trifoliata*	1	
480 Nutmeg do	*tenuifolia*	1	
481 Bird's nest do	*var.*	1	
482 Box leaved do	*tarentina*	2	
483 Chinese red flowered do	tomentosa		
484 Chinese garden nandina	Nandina domestica	2	
485 Single red oleander	Nerium oleander		50
486 white do	*v. albo*	1	
487 flesh coloured do	*v. carnea*	1	
488 yellow do	*v. lutea*	2	
489 Double variegated do	*v. variegata*	1	
490 splendid do	*v. splendens*	2	
491 Gold striped leaved do	*v. fol. varieg.*	2	
492 Chinese double white nerium	coronarium	3	
493 Ogeche lime	Nyssa candicans	1	
494 Great tupelo	tomentosa	1	
495 European olive	Olea europæa	1	
496 Large seeded do	*v. macrocarpa*	1	
497 Small do do	*v. microcarpa*	1	50
498 Long leaved do	*v. longifolia*	2	
499 Box leaved do	*v. buxifolia*		
500 American do	americana	1	
501 Chinese fragrant do	fragrans	2	
502 Madeira laurel leaved do	excelsa	5	
503 Asiatic, *or cape do*	capensis		
504 Star of Bethlehem, *see page* 94.	Ornithogalum		
505 Variegated oxalis	Oxalis versicolor		50
506 Yellow do	lutea		50
507 Rose coloured do	rosacea		50
508 Purple do	purpurea		50
509 Hairy do	hirta		50
510 Sessile leaved do	sessilifolia		50

K

511	Chinese purple sweet pæony tree	Pæonia moutan	$ 5
512	rose coloured do	v. rosea	5
513	white and purple do	p. papaveracea	25
514 *	white herbaceous pæony	sinensis, *Whitleii*	5
515 *	crimson do	v. Humei	8
516 *	rose scented do	v. fragrans	10
517	Sea pancratium	Pancratium maritimum	75
518	Carolina do	carolinianum	50
519	Illyrian do	illyricum	1
520	Fan leaved do	littorale	
521	Caribean do	caribæum	
523	Heart leaved do	amboinense	
524	Blue passion flower	Passiflora cerulea	1
525	Rose coloured do	incarnata	1
526	Yellow do	lutea	1
527	Palmated do	palmata	1
528	Hairy do	hirsuta	1
529	Orange do	aurantia	
530	Splendid do	racemosa	
531	Bitten leaved pavonia	Pavonia præmorsa	2
532	Pennyroyal, or rasp leaved *geranium*	Pelargonium radula	75
533	Otto of rose scented do	v. odorata	50
534	Dwarf do do	v. minor	50
535	Crimson horse-shoe do	zonale	50
536	Scarlet do do	v. coccinea	75
537	Flame coloured do do	v. flammea	1
538	Flesh coloured do do	v. carnea	75
539	White do do	v. alba	1
540	Double scarlet do do	v. pleno	2
541	Silver edged do do	v. fol. marginata	75
542	Bath scarlet do	var.	75
543	Great mallow leaved do	macrophyllum	2
544	Scarlet flowering do	inquinans	50
545	Bright scarlet do	v. coccinea	50
546	Curled leaved do do	v. crispa	50
547	Striped leaved do do	v. fol. variegato	50
548	Birch leaved do	betulinum	75
549	Heart leaved do	cordatum	75
550	Splendid do	speciosum	1
551	Nutmeg scented do	fragrans	50
552	Apple scented do	odoratissimum	50

553 Balm scented geranium	Pelargonium vitifolium	$0	50
554 Palmated balm do	v. *palmatum*		75
555 Rose scented do	capitatum		50
556 Scentless do	v. *inodorum*		50
557 Great white flowering do	grandiflorum	1,	
558 Oak leaved do	quercifolium		50
559 Plain oak leaved do	v. *minor*		75
560 Fair Helen do	v. *minima*	1	
561 Velvet leaved, *or pep-* } *permint scented do* }	tomentosum		75
562 Ivy leaved do	peltatum		75
563 Citron, *or bergamot* } *scented do* }	citriodorum		75
564 Sorrel leaved do	acetosum		75
565 Burnished do	ardens	1	
566 Night smelling do	triste	1	
567 Tuberous rooted do	tuberosum	1	
568 Ladies mantle leaved do	alchemilloides		75
569 Anemone leaved do	anemonifolium		50
570 Strawberry do	fragaroides		50
571 Glutinous do	glutinosum		75
572 Banbury's do	banburiense	2	
573 Cleopatra do	cleopatrium	2	
574 Triumphant do	triumphans	2	
575 Prince Regent do	regium	3	
576 August flowering do	augustum	2	
577 Rowena do	Rowanii	2	
578 Hooded leaved do	cucullatum	1	
579 Betony leaved do	betonicum	1	
580 Jagged leaved do	lacerum		
581 Purple flowered do	purpurascens	1	
582 Chandler's royal purple do	v. *splendens*	2	
583 Superb flowered do	formosum superbum	2	
584 Lady Barrington's do	Barringtonii	2	
585 Gouty stalked do	gibbosum	1	
586 Thorny do	spinosum		
587 Commander-in-Chief do	var.	2	
588 Blucher do	var.	2	
589 Fiery flowered do	ignescens	2	
590 Square stalked do	tetragonum		
591 Tricoloured do	tricolor		
592 Maple leaved do	acerifolium		
593 Murray's do	Murrayana	2	
594 Davy's do	Davyana	2	

595 Red flowered geranium	Pelargonium rubescens	$2
596 Botany-Bay do	australe	1
597 Reniform leaved do	reniformis	1
598 Sage leaved phlomis	Phlomis fruticosa	1
599 Orange coloured do	leonurus	1
600 New-Zealand flax	Phormium tenax	2
601 Heath leaved phylica	Phylica ericoides	1
602 Privet leaved phillyrea	Phillyrea media	1
603 Olive leaved do	oleæfolia	1
604 Narrow leaved do	angustifolia	2
605 Broad leaved do	latifolia	1
606 Variegated leaved do	v. fol. varieg.	1 50
607 Rose coloured pimelea	Pimelea rosea	
608 Georgia bark tree	Pinckneya pubescens	1
609 Black-pepper tree	Piper nigrum	
610 Officinal pistachia nut	Pistachia trifolia	2
611 Chinese fragrant pittosporum	Pittosporum tobira	$ 1 to 2
612 Wave leaved do	undulatum	
613 Leathery leaved do	coriaceum	
614 Rose coloured leadwort	Plumbago rosea	1
615 Dark flowered do	tristis	1
616 Red flowered plumeria	Plumeria rubra	
617 Silky leaved podalyria	Podalyria sericea	1
618 Storax leaved do	styracifolia	1
619 Tuberose, *see page 96.*	Polyanthes tuberosa	
620 Great flowering portlandia	Portlandia grandiflora	5
621 *Auricula) for many (	Primula auricula	
622 *Polyanthus > varieties <	polyanthus	
623 *Primrose) see p. 56. (	vulgaris, &c.	
624 English laurel	Prunus lauro-cerasus	75
625 Striped do	v. fol. varieg.	1
626 Portugal do	lusitanica	1
627 Carolina wild orange	caroliniensis	1
628 Fruit bearing pomegranate	Punica granatum	50
629 Double flowering do	v. pleno	50
630 White do do	v. albo	1
631 Yellow do do	v. flava	1
632 Dwarf profuse do do	nana	75
633 *Scarlet flowering Japan apple	Pyrus japonica	1
634 *White do do	v. albo	2
635 *Ranunculus, *see page* 89.	Ranunculus	

636 Silver striped buckthorn	Rhamnus alaturnus, *fol. var.*		$2
637 Tea buckthorn of China	theezans		
638 Striped rose bay	Rhododendron ponticum, *fol. var.*		2
639 Chinese rèd lac	Rhus succedanum		
640 Shining capè sumach	lucidum	2	
641 Smooth rivina	Rivina lævis	1	
642 Chinese robinia	Robinia chamlagu	2	
643 *Red China everblooming rose	Rosa indica		62
644 *Blueish marbled do	v. *cerulea*		75
645 Single velvet do	semperflorens	1	
646 Purple velvet, *or Otaheite do*	v. *pleno*		62
647 Blush changeable do	*diversiflora*	1	
648 Hundred leaved do	*centifolia*	1	
649 Tea scented do. *of exquisite fragrance*	*odorata*	2	
650 Dwarf, *or pompone, very small and delicate*	*minor*	1	
651 Dark crimson do	*sanguinea*		75
652 Semidouble purple do, *variegated*	*purpurea*	1	50
653 Bichonia do	*bichonia*	1	50
654 Resplendent do	*resplendens*	1	50
655 Amaranthus do	*amaranthiflora*	2	
656 White and red do	*subalba*	1	
657 Lord Macartney's white do	bracteata	2	
658 Three leaved single do	sinica	2	
659 Miss Lawrence's do. *the smallest and most delicate of all roses**	Lawrencia	2	
660 Evergreen do	lævigata	1	
661 Lady Banks's do	Banksiæ		
662 Persian do	berberifolia		50
663 Rosemary	Rosmarinus officinalis		
664 Double rose leaved bramble	Rubus rosæfolius, *pl.*	1	
665 Ruscus, *see page* 44.	Alexandrian laurel		
666 Scarlet flowered sage	Salvia coccinea		50

* So called in London in honour of Miss Lawrence, of that city, authoress of a splendid work on this delightful class of plants.

667 India soapberry	Sapindus saponaria	$1
668 *Chinese strawberry saxifrage	Saxifragà sarmentosa	50
669 *Scarlet fruited schisandra	Schisandra coccinea	1
670 Squill, *see page* 95.	Scilla	
671 Tree houseleek	Sempervivum arboreum	1
672 Cape Septas	Septas capensis	3
673 Japan box thorn	Serissa fætida	1
674 Double flowered do do	*v. pleno*	1
675 Shrubby Sicilian catchfly	Silene fruticosa	1
676 Striped star grass	Sisyrinchium striatum	1
677 Peruvian winter cherry	Solanum quercifolium	1
678 Carolina do	caroliniense	50
679 Japan sophora	Sophora japonica	2
680 Cape sophora	capensis	3
681 Wing podded do	tetraptera	2
682 African sparmannia	Sparmannia africana	1 50
683 Variegated stapelia	Stapelia variegata	75
684 Three pointed do	trisulca	1
685 Beautiful do	pulchella	1
686 Great flowered do	grandiflora	1
687 Star flowering do. &c.	radiata, &c.	1
688 Chinese sterculea	Sterculea platanifolia	1
689 Chinese tallow tree	Stillingia sebifera	1
690 Queen's strelitz, *very splendid*	Strelitzia reginæ	15
691 Three flowered styphelia	Styphelia triflora	
692 Chinese yew	Taxus macrophylla	2
693 Splendid warratah	Telopea speciosissima	
694 Shrubby germander	Teucrium fruticans	1
695 Green tea	Thea viridis	3
696 Bohea tea	bohea	3
697 Fragrant thunbergia	Thunbergia fragrans	
698 Purple leaved tradescantia	Tradescantia discolor	3
699 *Heliotrope scented colt's foot	Tussilago.fragrans	1
700 European furze	Ulex europæus	50
701 Chinese urena	Urena lobata	
702 Lemon scented verbena	Verbena triphylla	1
703 Laurustinus	Viburnum tinus	1
704 Shining leaved do	*v. lucidum*	
705 Striped leaved do	*v. fol. varieg.*	1
706 Chinese laurel leaved viburnum	laurifolium	

707 Scarlet Madagascar periwinkle	} Vinca rosea	$0	50
708 White do do	v. alba		50
709 *Fragrant double violet	Viola odoratissima		50
710 Double purple violet	v. purpurea		50
711 Double Japan volkameria	Volkameria japonica	1	
712 Panicled wachendorfia	Wachendorfia paniculata	1	
713 Thyrse flowered do	thyrsiflora	1	
714 Hairy do	hirsuta	1	
715 Pyramidal Watsonia	Watsonia rosea	1	
716 New-Holland westringia	Westringia rosmarinacea		
717 Adam's needle	Yucca gloriosa	1	
718 Recurved leaved do	recurvifolia	2	
719 Narrow leaved do	draconis	2	
720 *Adam's thread	filamentosa	1	

AGRICULTURAL AND GARDEN SEEDS

Of the various kinds, in wholesale quantities, will be supplied on the usual terms.

W. P.

A SHORT TREATISE

On the management of Fruit and Ornamental Trees, Shrubs, Plants, &c. with cursory descriptions of some which are of recent introduction and acknowledged merit.

THE proprietor of the LINNÆAN GARDEN, in supplying the orders for Trees, &c. from remote parts of the United States, having frequent applications for directions for their management to accompany them, concludes that the following brief remarks will be found acceptable.

Season for Transplanting.

Spring is the season when we feel the most pleasure in making our rural improvements, and from this circumstance probably it has become the most general season for planting trees—but experience has proved the fall planting to be the most successful, especially in those parts of the United States which are subject to droughts, as the trees planted in autumn suffer little or none from a drought, when those set out in spring often perish in consequence of it.

Trees, &c. on their arrival at the place of destination.

As soon as the trees arrive at the place where they are to be planted, let a trench be dug in cultivated ground, the bundles unpacked, and the roots well wet and immediately covered with earth in the trench, observing to make the earth fine that is spread over them, so as not to leave vacancies for the admission of air to dry the roots—it having been found by experience that the thriftiness of trees, the first season after transplantation, depends much on the fine fibres of the roots being kept moist, and not suffered to dry from the time they are taken up until they are replanted—a precaution which is always attended to with respect to the trees sent from this garden, as the roots are invariably kept moist from the time they are taken up until they are packed ready to be shipped. Their success, therefore, must depend principally on the subsequent management on their arrival at the place of destination, for if, when the bundles are unpacked, the trees are carelessly left exposed to drying winds, the young fibres of the roots must perish, and the trees, if they live at all, cannot thrive the first season, as they can receive little or no nourishment until those fibres are replaced.

Manner of Planting.

Let the holes be dug somewhat larger than is sufficient to admit the roots in their natural position, and of sufficient depth to allow the tree to be placed two or three inches deeper than it was before transplanting—take care to cut off any wounded parts of the root, and to reduce the top full one third, by shortening the branches, or thinning them out. Let from two to four shovels full of well rotted stable manure, in proportion to the size of the tree, be incorporated with the earth, and the whole made fine previous to filling it in ; and, during the operation of filling in the earth, let the tree be several times shaken, in order that the soil may be admitted among the finer roots, and when completely filled up, let the ground be well trodden down, and finish by making a hollow or basin around the tree, to catch the rain and convey it to the roots, or to receive the watering which it will be necessary to give it should the season prove dry.

To cause the Trees to thrive.

The ground where they are planted must be kept cultivated—young trees will not thrive if the grass is permitted to form a sod around them ; and if it should be necessary to plant them in grass ground, care must be taken to keep the earth mellow and free from grass for three or four feet distant around them, and, every autumn, some well rotted manure should be dug in around each tree, and every spring the bodies of the Apple, Pear, Plum, and Cherry trees, and others that it is particularly desirable to promote the growth of, should be brushed over with common soft soap, undiluted with water—this treatment will give a thriftiness to the trees surpassing the expectation of any one, who has not witnessed its effect. Should the first season after transplanting prove dry, regular waterings will be necessary, and from a neglect of proper attention in this respect, many lose a large portion of their trees during a drought.

Soil, Culture, &c.

APPLES.

Rich strong loams are the soils most conducive to the growth of the Apple—the roots of Apple trees being more horizontal than perpendicular, they require a soil less deep than the Pear, and it is on this account that moist soils are more requisite for the Apple, as the roots, extending themselves near the surface, are not benefitted by the moisture, which is found at a greater distance from the surface of the earth. Apple orchards will, however, succeed on any soil except a quicksand or a cold clay, if proper attention is paid to keeping the ground in constant cultivation, and manure is regularly dug or ploughed in around the trees. Old well rotted stable manure, decomposed vegetable mould from swamps or woods, and river mud, have been found most suitable for this purpose.

PEARS.

These require a deep light soil, in which their perpendicular roots can easily penetrate—clay, compact, cold, and wet soils, do not suit their growth. When the roots of the Pear penetrate so as to reach the water, the branches become long and slender, and the leaves narrow, changing speedily to a yellowish appearance, and the ends of the branches often perish as if burned. With regard to manuring and keeping the ground cultivated, the Pear requires the same attention as that prescribed for the Apple. This tree is, however, subject to one malady peculiar to itself, commonly called the *Fire Blight, or Brulere*, which attacks trees in the most flourishing state, generally commencing at the top or extremity of the branches, and extending downwards. This is caused by a stroke of the sun, which extracts the sap from the uppermost branches of the tree, or from such as are most exposed to its influence, with more rapidity than it can be replaced; or from powerful rays of the sun heating the bark to such a degree as to arrest or nullify the progress of the sap. It is therefore recommended to plant trees in Pear orchards much closer than in those of the Apple. The only remedy against these attacks is to immediately saw off the branches one or two feet below where the blight extends, in which case they generally revive.

PEACHES.

The preferable soil for a Peach orchard is a rich sandy loam, but this fruit will succeed in any soil with proper attention to cultivation and manuring; particular care, however, should be taken not to plant a new orchard on the site of an old one. It may be necessary also to remark, that the ground where they are planted should be kept in a constant state of cultivation, as they become bark-bound and unthrifty the second year after the grass has formed a sod around them. There are two causes which have operated against the success of this tree, and which seem peculiar to it—the one is a *Worm* which attacks the tree at the root, near the surface of the ground, and often totally encircles it; the other is a disease usually denominated the *Yellows*.

The Worm.—The most proper course to obviate the depredations of the worm is to examine the trees every spring and autumn, and to make an application of a mixture of fresh cow dung and clay to the wounds which have been made by them. Lime or ashes thrown around the roots of Peach trees are found to prevent, in a great measure, the depredations of the worm.

Yellows.—This disease, which commenced its ravages in New-Jersey and Pennsylvania about the year 1797, and in New-York in 1801, and has spread through several of the states, is by far more destructive to Peach trees than the worm, and is evidently contagious. The disease is spread at the time when the trees are in bloom, and is disseminated by the pollen or farina blowing from the flowers of diseased trees, and impregnating the flowers of those which are healthy, and which is quickly circulated by the sap through the branches, foliage, and fruit, causing the fruit, wherever the infection extends, to ripen prematurely. That this disease is entirely distinct from the *worm*, is sufficiently proved by the circumstance, that Peach trees which have been inoculated on Plum or Almond stocks, though never affected by the *worm*, are equally subject to the *yellows*—and a decisive proof of its being contagious is, that a healthy tree, inoculated from a branch of a diseased one, instead of restoring it to vigour and health, immediately becomes itself infected with the disease. As all efforts to totally subdue it must require a long course of time, the best method to pursue towards its eventual eradication, is to stop its progress, and prevent its farther extension—to accomplish which, the following means are recommended, which have been found particularly successful in the orchards of the proprietor, as well as in those of others in his neighbourhood, which continue to produce fruit of the finest quality and in the greatest abundance.

As soon as a tree is discovered to possess the characteristics of the disease, which is generally known by the leaves putting on a sickly yellow appearance—but of which the premature ripening of the fruit is a decisive proof—it should be marked, so as to be removed the ensuing autumn, which must be done without fail, for if left again to bloom, it would impart the disease to many others in its vicinity; care is also necessary, in its removal, to take out all the roots of the diseased tree, especially if another is to be planted in the same place, so that the roots of the tree to be planted may not come in contact with any of those of the one which was diseased.

If your neighbour has trees infected with the yellows in a quarter contiguous to your's, it will be necessary to prevail on him to remove them, that your's may not be injured by them. By being thus particular in speedily removing such trees as may be infected, the disease is prevented from extending itself to the rest of the orchard, and the residue will consequently be preserved in perfect health at the trifling loss of a few trees annually from a large orchard. And here it may be well to remark, that the propagation of the Peach on Plum stocks will only answer where the trees are to be trained as Dwarfs, as it is found that in standard Peaches on Plum stocks, the Peach is apt to overgrow the Plum, and the latter being unable to furnish a sufficient portion of sap to promote the growth of the former, the Peach becomes stinted and short lived; and Duhammel, the most able French writer on the culture of fruits, pronounces the Plum stock never to be eligible for Peach trees which are intended as standards.

CHERRIES.

Cherry trees will not succeed in a low wet situation; they thrive best in a rich sandy loam, and the soil around them must be kept cultivated until they have attained a considerable size. If the bodies of the trees become bark-bound, some rotten manure must be dug in around them, and the bodies and largest branches be brushed over with soft soap. Tho Morello cherry having become almost extinct in some parts of the United States, in consequence of an insect which perforates the branches, and produces large excrescences, which, unless lopped off as soon as they appear, soon destroy the tree altogether—it may be satisfactory to state that the English Morello, and the Plumstone Morello, are not subject to this disease—and that the fruit of both of these kinds is far superior in size and flavour to the common Morello, and ripens equally late in the season.

PLUMS, APRICOTS, AND NECTARINES.

For these a light rich soil is preferable, and the same care is necessary as has been recommended for fruit trees generally, in keeping the ground cultivated around them when young; for although it is a common observation, that Plum trees succeed best in a hard trodden soil, and though such a situation may cause the trees to retain their fruit, still it must be decidedly unfavourable to their growth. Plums, Apricots, and Nectarines, are smooth skinned fruit, and are in some parts of the United States subject to be injured by a small bug called the *Curculio*, which stings the fruit, and causes it to drop before it has attained its proper size. Their depredations may be effectually prevented by paving round the trees *as far as the branches extend*, as it has been incontestibly proved by frequent experiments made by the proprietor of this garden, and others, that the *Curculio* will not infest those trees where they cannot find means of immediately concealing themselves in the ground on dropping from the branches. Plum trees are also subject to injury from another insect, which stings the branches, and causes large protuberances to form on them, which, if not cut off, produce a canker that in time destroys the tree. There are some kinds, however, which are not subject to the attacks of this insect, viz. the Chicasaw, Early Coral, Golden Drop, and other native Plums, the Cherry Plum, Bolmer's Washington, Flushing Gage, and Yellow Egg Plums.—And here I will remark, that Duhammel, the highest authority on the cultivation of fruits, recommends Peach stocks as preferable to all others for the free growing kinds of Plums—such as the Green Gage, &c. &c.—as the additional quantity of sap furnished by the Peach stock very much accelerates the growth of the Plum. Still it is necessary, in order to guard against the worm, that they should be grafted beneath the surface of the ground, which, however, is the practice usually pursued.

FIGS.

In the middle and northern states, where the Fig trees are killed nearly to the ground by the severity of the winters, two crops of fruit may be obtained each season by planting the early kinds in a warm or sheltered situation, if pains are taken in autumn to bend the trees down, and cover them with earth, sloping the embankment so as to cast off the rain;

L

but, early in April, they should be uncovered and set upright. By this treatment they will produce one crop of fruit early in the summer, and another in September or October.

GRAPES.

Of all the fruits cultivated in the United States, there is none more generally esteemed than the Grape; yet, in the middle and northern states, this fruit is seldom met with in perfection but in cities. The proprietor having attended particularly to the cultivation of the Grape for nearly twenty years past, can confidently assure those who wish to have this fruit in perfection, that they may depend on their vines producing well if they will attend to the following directions; for although a season may sometimes occur when the cold and wet will retard the ripening of the fruit, yet even in the worst seasons a tolerable crop may be calculated on.

There are two causes why the cultivation of the vine has not been successful in the *country*, attention to which is indispensably necessary; *the first* is the proper selection of those kinds which are suitable to the climate, and which come to perfection by the middle or end of September; *the second* is the want of attention to the culture requisite for ripening the wood, which in cities is effected by the dry warm air with little or no care, but in the country, art and attention are required to produce the desired effect. I have, therefore, given the following list of Grapes, with brief descriptions of their qualities, &c. and by reference to page 30, it will be found which are suitable for the *country*, and which will only succeed in the *city*, or in Grape houses roofed with glass.

1. *Raisin précoce de la Madeleine.*—This Grape has small bunches, the berries are also small, and of a dark violet colour, of inferior flavour, and principally desirable for their early maturity; ripens in August.

2. *Early White Muscadine, or Summer Sweet Water.*—This is a round Grape, with a thin skin, and of a delicate flavour. It is a great bearer, and resembles the White Sweet Water in almost every respect, except that it ripens much earlier, being usually in perfection from the 20th to the end of August.

3. *July Grape, Early Black Cluster, or Morillon noir hatif.*—This is a small round fruit, of pleasant flavour, and grows in very compact bunches; it is a good bearer, and ripens in August.

4. *Large Black Cluster.*—This is larger than the above; its juice, however, is rather harsh, and less agreeable to the taste than the preceding one; it is said that this is the Grape from which Port Wine is made; it ripens early in September.

5. *Small Black Cluster, or Burgundy.*—This has oval berries, and is a very pleasant fruit; ripens in September.

6. *Miller's Burgundy, Black Cluster, or Meunier.*—This is a small black Grape, rather of an oval form, and grows in short compact bunches; the juice is sweet and pleasant; it is a great bearer, and a good Grape for Wine; ripens in September.

7. *Auvergne, Pineau, or True Burgundy, sometimes called Bourguignon.*—This is rather an indifferent fruit for the table, but in Europe considered one of the best for making Wine; it is of a middle size, and somewhat oval; ripens in September.

8. *White Sweet Water.*—This has very large round white berries close on the bunch, which is of a good size, the skin and flesh are very delicate, and replete with very agreeable juice; the berries on the sides of the branches next the sun are often clouded with spots of a russet colour. This Grape flourishes admirably in our cities, where large quantities are annually sold in the shops; some bunches which grew in the garden of Edward Probyn, Esq. during the summer of 1821, were of uncommon size, one of which weighed 1 *lb.* 10 *oz.* and was 17 inches in girth; in fine seasons it succeeds in the country also.

9. *Black Sweet Water.*—This is a roundish fruit, growing in small compact bunches, is very sweet, and ripens in September.

10. *Black Madeira.*—This Grape I received direct from Madeira; it produces abundantly, and is one of those that agree best with our climate; the fruit is very jucy and of a pleasant flavour, and seems well calculated both for Wine and the table; it ripens in August.

11. *Purple Madeira.*—This is a small pale purple Grape, loosely set on long bunches; they have a vinous perfume and flavour when ripe, but are not suitable for the table.

12. *Bordeaux Purple.*—This Grape I received direct from Bordeaux a few years since; it produces very abundantly, and the fruit, which is round, is of a pleasant flavour and very juicy, though but of a middle size; it ripens early in September.

13. *White Frontignac, or Muscat blanc de Frontignan.*—This has large long bunches of a conical form, berries round

and very close; colour white, skin thick, juice luscious and musky, and of exquisite flavour; perhaps no Grape is superior to this as a table fruit; ripens in September.

14. *Grizzly Frontignac.*—The berries are round, tolerably large, colour brown red and yellow intermixed, and they have a high musky perfumed flavour; ripens in September.

15. *Black Frontignac, or Muscat noir.*—This has very large round fruit, covered with a meally bloom, and of a very fine flavour. It is called, at the Cape of Good Hope, *the Black Constantia;* ripens in September.

16. *Red Frontignac, or Muscat rouge.*—Berries less close than No. 13, and of a less size, colour lively red, skin thin, and of a musky flavour; ripens better than the white, but is not equal to it; ripe in September.

17. *Blue, or Violet Frontignac, or Muscat violet.*—The bunches of this Grape are small, the berries are also small and loosely set, and of a black colour, powdered with a fine violet bloom, and possess a most delicious flavour; ripens in September.

18. *White Muscat of Alexandria, or Alexandrian Frontignac.*—The bunches are long, the berries not closely set, but large, oval, and yellow, and of a very fine musky flavour.

19. *White Chasselas, Royal Muscadine, D'Arboyce, or Chasselas blanc.*—This has round amber coloured berries, of moderate size, thin skin, and soft juicy flesh; the bunches are very large, and frequently weigh from six to seven pounds.

20. *Red Chasselas, or Chasselas rouge.*—This is very like the above in size and shape, but of a dark red colour; it is a good Grape, but ripens later than the white.

21. *Musk Chasselas, Chasselas musqué, or Frankindale.*—This has a large round green berry, sweet, and of a musky flavour.

22. *Black Hamburg.*—The berries are large, black, and inclining to an oval; they hang loosely on the bunches, which are well formed; the skin is thick, but the flavour good, and it is a great bearer, on which account it is much esteemed; ripens in September.

23. *Red Hamburg, or Gibraltar.*—The berries are dark red, skin thick, flesh juicy and delicate, the shape of the berry and form of the bunch both resemble the foregoing.

24. *Parsley leaved, Cioutat, or Raisin d'Autriche.*—This is a variety of the Chasselas, with leaves finely divided, but of which the bunches and fruit are rather smaller; the flavour is fine, the skin thin, and the flesh delicate and juicy.

25. *French Chocolate coloured.*—This was received from France about thirty years since ; the vine is of very vigorous growth, and a great bearer, and seems to suit our climate well, and to be as hardy as our native wild Grapes ; the fruit is oval, of a sprightly flavour, and the bunches large ; it is an excellent Wine Grape, as well as an agreeable one for the table ; it ripens from the middle to the end of September.

26. *Red Muscadel.*—The berries are very large, oval, of an equal size throughout the bunch, and of a beautiful red colour ; the skin is thick, and the flesh hard ; the bunches frequently weigh from five to six pounds.

27. *White, or true Tokay.*—The berries are somewhat oval, and closely set on the bunch, which is of moderate size, the skin is thin, and the flesh delicate, abounding with very agreeable juice.

28. *Lombardy, flame coloured Tokay, or Rhenish.*—The berries are large, oval, and of a fine flame colour, the bunches regularly formed with shoulders, and frequently arrive to the weight of six or seven pounds.

29. *Malvoisie, Malmsey, or Blue Tokay.*—This has small berries, rather oval, and of a brown colour, powdered with a blue bloom ; the skin is thin, the flesh delicate, and replete with vinous juice.

30. *St. Peter's, or Saint Pierre.*—A large, and very fine black fruit, of a somewhat oval form ; the skin is thin, the flesh very delicate and juicy, and the bunches large.

31. *Bland's Grape.*—This is a round fruit, of a pale red colour, middle size, and very pleasant flavour ; it is an agreeable table fruit, and is also said to make excellent Wine. It has been supposed for many years to be a native of Virginia, but I have recently received information, which cannot be doubted, through Doctor Norton, of Richmond, that this Grape was introduced many years since into Virginia from Italy, by a Mr. Mazzei, and carried thence to Philadelphia by Mr. Bland, and indeed the general aspect of the plant proves it to be an Exotic Grape.

32. *White Cornishon, or Cornishon blanc.*—The berries are very long, and swelled in the middle, not closely set on the bunches, but white, sweet, and excellent.

33. *Syrian.*—The berries are large, white, and oval ; skin thick, flesh firm, and the bunches well formed and enormously large, sometimes weighing above twelve pounds, and making a most beautiful appearance. Although this Grape is inferior to some others, still, as it is very prolific, it merits a place in every collection.

34. *Isabella Grape.*— This is an American Grape, a native of Dorchester, South-Carolina, and was introduced to this state by Mrs. Isabella Gibbs, the lady of George Gibbs, Esq. of St. Augustine, who then resided at Brooklyn, Long-Island, and in honour of that lady has been called *Isabella Grape.* It is a dark purple fruit, of a good size, oval form, and juicy, and nearly equals some of the European kinds; and, for vigour of growth, and an abundant yield, exceeds any other yet cultivated in this country, and requires no protection during the winter season. General Joseph Swift, of New-York, informed me, that a single vine in his garden produced above eight bushels during each of the seasons of 1820 and 1821. This Grape promises to rival all others in cultivation in this country for the purpose of making Wine, as it possesses all the requisites to ensure success in making Wine of a fair quality, or for making Brandy equal to that of France; it ripens in September.

35. *Scuppernon.*—This Grape has been cultivated with great success in North-Carolina, of which state it is a native, and where many hogsheads of Wine are annually made from it. The Wine is of a very agreeable and peculiar flavour. It will no doubt be ere long cultivated extensively throughout the United States for the purpose of making Wine, as the experiments in North-Carolina, which, in some cases, have been on quite an extensive scale, have realized the most sanguine wishes of those who commenced the undertaking.

36. *Alexander's, or Schuylkill Muscadel.*—This Grape, which has been erroneously called at the Spring Mill Vineyard, and at Philadelphia, the *Constantia*, or *Cape of Good Hope* Grape, is unquestionably a native of our own country, and originated in the vicinity of Philadelphia. The berries are black, very sweet, and of a slight musky flavour, but contain a pulp. Wine of a fair quality has been made from this Grape in different sections of the Union; and Mr. Adlum, of the District of Columbia, has succeeded in making a Wine from it very similar to Burgundy.

37. *Orwigsburg.*—This is a native white Grape, sweet, with a thin skin, and larger than the *Meunier;* it is very hardy, yields abundantly, and is highly esteemed even by connoisseurs. I am informed, by Doctor William E. Hulings, of Philadelphia, (a gentleman distinguished for his philanthropy and for his zeal in introducing to notice such fruits as promise permanent advantage to our country,) that this Grape was discovered about three miles from the town of Orwigs-

burg, in Pennsylvania, and by him named after the place of
its origin; ripens early in September.

38. *Elsingburg.*—For the dissemination of this Grape, we
are also indebted to Doctor Hulings, of Philadelphia, who
brought it about seven years since from Salem county, New-
Jersey. The berries are blue, large, and juicy, and it promises to be an excellent Wine Grape, the vine is also extremely hardy; ripens early in September.

39 and 40. These two varieties of the Grape, *(see page
32)* which are said to be very fine, and to succeed admirably, I
received from my valued correspondent, Doctor Norton, of
Richmond, whose acute observation and zeal in bringing
meritorious fruits into notice, promises much benefit to our
country—to one, which was discovered in Prince Edward
county, Virginia, he has given the name of *Prince Edward
Grape*—to the other, which is a seedling from Bland's
Grape, and for bringing which into notice our country is
particularly indebted to Doctor Norton, I have given the
name of *Norton's Virginia Seedling*—both kinds are now
under successful cultivation.

The great object being to introduce into cultivation, in the
middle states, those Grapes whose character particularly as-
similates to the climate, and such as come to maturity not
later than the month of September, I shall receive an acces-
sion to the extensive catalogue, found at page 30, during the
present autumn, (1823,) of the following varieties, which are
the most celebrated kinds, cultivated in France for Wine
and the table, *in the latitude of Paris,* and orders therefor
can be supplied in the autumn of 1824 :—

91 *Murlot, or Languedoc*
92 *Bourguignon, or Plant de Roi*
93 *Bourguignon blanc, or feuille ronde*
94 *Meslier*
95 *Petit Muscadet, or pineau-gris*
96 *Mansard*
97 *Bourguignon noir, or petit-goy*
98 *Rochelle noir*
99 *Saint Morillo, or gris mélé*
100 *L'éricé noir, or liverdum*
101 *Panse musquée*
102 *Malvoisie blanche du Po—and about twenty other
varieties.*

CULTIVATION OF GRAPES.

Soil and Situation.

The Grape delights in a deep light soil, where the roots can penetrate to a great depth with perfect facility. It flourishes in gravelly soils, where the land is rich and not heavy, and will even scarcely fail to grow vigourously in any land except a hard clay. The ground should, however, be made perfectly mellow to the depth of two feet, and if not naturally rich, should be made so with old well rotted stable or cowyard manure, the latter always preferable. The situation should have a southern aspect; an eastern aspect is found to render the fruit and foliage most liable to mildew, and a southwest exposure is found to be preferable to all others.

Transplanting.

Either the spring or autumn answer for transplanting vines, but the latter is the preferable season. In removing the vines it is necessary to keep the roots moist from the time they are taken up until replanted. Let the holes be dug eighteen inches deep, and some well rotted cow-yard or stable manure be incorporated with the earth that is filled in around them, and let them be watered as soon as they are planted.

Pruning.

About the first week in November it will be necessary to prune the vines; if they are quite young, the branches of the same season's growth should be trimmed down to about four buds, but, as the vines advance in age and size, the number of buds to be left may be increased, and when the vines are quite strong, some of the most vigourous shoots may be left from four to six feet in length; observing always in pruning to proportion the number of buds left to the strength of the shoot. In the spring many unnecessary shoots will be produced, which must be rubbed off, as they would exhaust the vine, and lessen the quantity and quality of the fruit; indeed, care should be taken to rub off all such buds as are unnecessary to furnish bearing shoots for the ensuing year, and to lop off such lateral branches as would tend to draw the sustenance from the main shoots.

Training.

Lattice fences, five feet high, and at a distance of six feet from each other, answer extremely well for vines, which should be planted along them at the distance of six feet asunder. On these fences the shoots should be trained in a horizontal or oblique direction, and each branch singly, so as to allow the air to pass freely through, and cause the wood to ripen well, on which invariably depends the success of the ensuing crop. At Thomery, a town near Paris, celebrated for its fine Grapes, the vines are trained on trellices eight feet high. These lattices possess this advantage, that the sun can shine on both sides of the vines in the course of the day, and that they allow a free passage to the air, which is of great benefit as well in maturing the fruit, as in ripening the wood. In some parts of France, however, where the culture of the vine is carried to so great an extent, a very simple mode is pursued, which is to place two poles to each vine, and to train up two shoots to each of the poles. This method might probably be found advantageous in this country on the principle of economy, when it is contemplated to establish extensive vineyards.

Culture, &c.

It is preferable in winter to protect most kinds of foreign Grapes in the following manner, though there are many which do not require it.:—In the course of the month of November, after they have been trimmed according to the above directions, bend each vine gently down, then stake it to keep it in its place ; after this, proceed to cover it with earth or litter, hilling the earth up well around, and sloping it to cast off the rain. In the beginning of April, they must be carefully uncovered, and trained along the lattices designed for them, or tied up to poles in such a way that the branches are kept separate from each other, and, if it is the first season after transplanting, allow but three or four of the most vigorous buds to grow, and rub off the others. It has been urged by some, that the necessity for covering most kinds of foreign vines precluded their culture for the purpose of making Wine; but it must have been unknown to them, that the vineyards on the Rhine, where large quantities of Wine are made, are treated in this manner. However, even this objection may be remedied by planting only those vines which are cultivated in the north of France, and which there withstand, without protection, a degree of cold full as great as that of the middle states; the new varieties which have originated in our own country bid fair also to do away every difficulty on this point. The ground around the vines must be kept mellow, and free from grass and weeds; and, every autumn, immediately after pruning them, it will be necessary to have from two to four shovels full of old well rotted manure dug in around each vine. It is to be understood that the directions for covering the vines during the winter, and the selection of early fruit, &c. are only necessary for the climate north of the Potomac; for in the more southern states, no protection of course is necessary, and all the later kinds of Grapes may be cultivated with every reasonable prospect of success; but all the other directions relative to pruning, training, manuring, &c. will be found necessary as well in a southern as in a northern clime.

GOOSEBERRIES.

This is a fruit generally planted, but from the necessary culture not being understood, few succeed in having them produce plentifully, and the fruit fair and of good size. To effect which, one third of the old wood must be regularly trimmed out every autumn, by which means a succession of thrifty bearing wood will be kept up, as the fruit is produced on the young shoots of the previous year's growth, and it is also necessary every autumn to dig in a plenty of old well rotted manure around them. This treatment will cause them to grow strong, and the fruit to be large and fair. In point of situation a northern aspect is preferable.

ORNAMENTAL FOREST TREES AND SHRUBS.

For all hardy Forest trees, except Evergreens, autumn is the preferable season for transplantation; if taken from a nursery, they are naturalized to an upland soil, but if taken from the woods or swamps, they should be planted in soil similar to that from which they are removed. Forest, as well as Fruit trees, to cause them to grow thrifty, require the ground to be kept cultivated around them; and when the bodies become bark-bound or mossy, they should be brushed over with soft soap, as directed for Fruit trees, especially the Mountain Ash, which sometimes becomes covered with white insects and their eggs; these should be scoured off first, before the soap is applied, or at the time of applying it.

WHITE CHINESE, or *Italian Mulberry*.

This is the species which has always been cultivated for rearing silk worms. It is originally from China, but, from being so extensively cultivated in Italy, it is more generally called the Italian Mulberry. This tree is very easy of cultivation, and of very rapid growth, and may be reared to any extent without difficulty, as it agrees so well with our climate, that they are found growing spontaneously in the hedges on Long-Island, from seeds which have been scattered by the winds or birds.

ENGLISH AND SPANISH FILBERTS.

These nuts, which are vended in large quantities in our markets, grow as well in our climate as the common hazelnut, and produce very abundantly. Such being the case, it is hoped, ere long, sufficient will be produced from our own soil to supersede the necessity of importation, as plantations of this tree would amply remunerate the possessor, or, if planted as a hedge, would be found to be very productive.

COMMON LOCUST.

Within a few years, many of our enterprizing landholders have been devoting their attention to planting extensive tracts with this tree, the wood of which is in so much request in ship building. An acre of these trees planted at two feet distant each way, will contain 10,890—at three feet distant, 4,840—and, at four feet distant, 2,722—and it is said no appropriation of land is more lucrative than that devoted to this purpose.

LIQUORICE.

The *Glycyrrhiza glabra*, or Liquorice, may be cultivated to equal perfection in the United States, as in any other country. It delights in a light rich sandy soil, and the product is so great, that it would yield an immense profit to the cultivator. Such being the case, it is to be hoped that the time is not far distant when we shall not have to depend on England and Spain for our supply.

DYER'S MADDER.

This plant, of so much importance in manufactures, and of which we have annually to import large quntities from Holland, will succeed in this country as well as in any part of Europe. It will thrive in any soil except a sand, and would amply remunerate those who would undertake its cultivation on a large scale, as the daily increase of our manufactories will cause an enlarged demand for this indispensable article.

ROSES.

No class of plants, so easy of culture as this, yields more intrinsic delights to the amateur; the diversity of size, colour, fragrance, and form, have been varied by art to an almost infinite degree, and in one collection alone in Europe, above 1200 varieties are enumerated. Enduring the rigour of the severest winters uninjured, and yielding with so little attention such a rich accumulation of beauty and fragrance, every garden should possess at least all the more conspicuous varieties of this unrivalled flower; and it is hoped ere long we shall see the fashion followed in this country, which has for years prevailed in England, of training the hardy varieties of the Chinese Everblooming Roses against the sides of our country houses and cottages, as the profusion of flowers which they daily afford from spring to autumn, gives to the retirement of these rural scenes a degree of Floral enchantment, and throws an air of magic round the spot.

YELLOW ROSES.

Some complain that the double yellow Roses do not flower well; it is therefore proper to remark, that they require an airy situation, and a light rich soil, and that every autumn one half of the old wood should be cut down within four inches of the ground; by this means a succession of thrifty blooming shoots will be kept up. The single yellow, and the red and yellow Austrian, it is well to treat in the same manner, though they bloom freely in almost any soil, and with little or no care.

EVERGREEN TREES AND SHRUBS.

These, if taken from the woods, should be planted in winter with balls of frozen earth; but, if taken from a nursery, where they have been naturalized to an upland soil, the preferable season is the spring, as many Evergreens fail when transplanted in autumn, especially if the earth falls entirely from the roots, and the frost penetrates to the earth below them when planted, which it seldom fails to do in the northern and middle states.

ASPARAGUS.

This plant, which is cultivated very extensively for the markets, requires that the soil be made very rich and light, and that it be made mellow to the depth of eighteen or twenty inches. The preferable mode of planting is in long narrow beds of about five feet wide, and the plants should be placed one foot apart each way in the beds.

STRAWBERRIES.

As beds of these generally want renewing every three or four years, it will be necessary in forming the new beds to select the plants in the proportion of nine bearing plants to one barren; and, in order to do this with certainty, it will be well to transplant them immediately after the fruit has matured. If, however, your beds are not encumbered with a superfluous number of barren plants, this precaution will not be indispensably necessary; though it is generally requisite with the English Hautboy, which is apt to produce a great proportion of barren plants, and even without proper attention, beds of this and of some other kinds will become almost totally unproductive.

CARNATION PINKS.

These should be covered in winter with a box or frame, or taken up with balls of earth, and planted during the winter under a common hot-bed, with or without glass, as they bear cold, but not cold and moisture at the same time.

GREEN-HOUSE PLANTS.

Among the plants which have hitherto been introduced to this country, none exceed those which have been received from China and Japan; in the former of which countries they are said to excel all other nations in the cultivation of flowers. It is also a happy circumstance, that nearly all the plants which have yet been received from either of those countries, are among the hardier kinds of Green-house plants, and succeed with very little attention; and, indeed, a number of them are found to withstand the winters of the middle states. It being, therefore, so desirable an object to obtain all the valuable plants of those countries, arrangements have been made to procure such as have already found their way to Europe, as well as to add annually to the collection by importations direct from China.

M

ORANGE AND LEMON TREES, &c.

The Orange, Lemon, Citron, Shaddock, and Lime are easily cultivated, and no trees will bear harder usage, if they are only secured from cold and frost. They may be removed every month in the year, and yet grow well with the aid of shade and moisture. Early in October they should be taken out of the boxes or pots in which they are growing, with the balls of earth entire, and have the sides and bottom shaved off about an inch deep with a sharp knife, to make room for fresh earth, and then replace them in the pots or boxes, first covering the holes at the bottom with shells or broken earthen, and some fresh compost; then fill in around the tree with the compost prepared as hereafter directed. If, in the course of replanting, the earth should have been much separated from the roots, the tree should be placed in a shady situation for a few days. If it is desirable to promote the growth, and to form large trees, then let boxes be made a size larger at every annual transplanting; but, if the boxes should be too large in proportion to the tree, fruit will not be produced so soon, nor in as great a quantity.

Compost for Orange Trees, and most other Green-House Plants.

Take one third good rich earth, one third well rotted stable manure, and one third swamp, or wood mould; but, where swamp mould cannot be procured, let two thirds be good rich earth; these must be well incorporated together, and, if mixed a few weeks previous to the time of using, it will be the better for it. This soil will suit all except Succulent Plants, such as the different species of Aloe, Cactus, Yucca, Stapelia, &c. which require a composition of half coarse sand, one fourth swamp mould, and one fourth common garden mould.

CAMELLIA JAPONICA, or Japan Rose.

Much as we are indebted to Japan and China for elegant plants, still we are more peculiarly so for the different species and varieties of the Camellia, which, for the many beauties it concentrates, may emphatically be styled " the Queen of Flowers." The different varieties of this plant form the most brilliant display of the Green-house from December to May, and the splendour of their flowers, and richness of their foliage, are surpassed by no others. The flowers of many of them equal in size the largest garden Rose, and combine a regularity of form, and richness of colouring, which present an admirable contrast with their dark shining green leaves, and render them the greatest ornaments of a room or the Green-house. They need less protection than almost any other Green-house plants, and four of them, which were left in the open ground during the winter of 1821, and which were protected merely by a hot-bed frame, received no injury, although the ground in the frame was frozen to the depth of five inches.

PÆONIA MOUTAN, or *Tree Pæony*.

In the gardens of China, they cultivate 240 varieties of this splendid plant, some of which are sold as high as a hundred ounces of gold; and in so much esteem is it held by them, that it is there called "the King of Flowers." During the months of March and April, this plant appears in its most magnificent garb, and its flowers, which are from eighteen inches to two feet in circumference, form, what is so rarely met with, a combination of splendour, delicacy, and fragrance. It is yet a rare plant, having been but recently introduced to this country; but, as it is one of the hardiest Green-house plants, it is very probable it may ultimately be found to stand our winters in the open air.

Besides the above we are indebted to China for three splendid Herbaceous Pæonies, viz.—

Pæonia sinensis Whitleii, with double white, or sulphureous yellow flowers, afterwards changing to white, and whose external petals are generally tinged with red; the stems are usually three feet high, with from two to three flowers on each.

Pæonia Humei, with very large double crimson flowers, of brilliant appearance, and a pleasant odour; flower stems also grow to the height of three feet.

Pæonia fragrans, with rose coloured sweet scented flowers; this blooms the latest of all, and the flowers are generally in cymes of two or three on a stem.

PYRUS JAPONICA, or *Scarlet Flowering Japan Apple*.

This is also a very desirable plant; its flowers, which are produced in clusters during most of the winter season, are of the most brilliant scarlet, and are succeeded by small fruit.

MAGNOLIA OBOVATA, *or Chinese Purple Magnolia.*

This plant is justly esteemed for the uncommon richness and beauty of its flowers, which are produced in March, and are of a delicate purple outside, and white within. All the other species of Chinese Magnolias are desirable plants, but more particularly the Magnolia conspicua, or Chandelier Magnolia, whose flowers are very splendid, and are also produced during the winter months.

GARDENIA FLORIDA, *or Cape Jasmine.*

This is also a justly admired plant; the bright shining green of its foliage, and the delightful odour of its large snow white flowers, which are produced from June to December, must ever render it one of the most esteemed exotics.

GORTERIA RIGENS, *or Starry Scarlet Gorteria.*

This, though it never attains a large size, is, notwithstanding, one of the most showy Green-house plants, as its flowers are large and brilliant. Its foliage, also, possesses a singularity, the under side of each leaf being white, with a stripe of green.

ROSA ODORATA, *Sweet China, or Tea Scented Rose.*

This is a most delightful plant, producing a greater abundance of flowers throughout the year than any other Rose, which are of the most exquisite fragrance, whereas most other Everblooming Roses have little or no scent.

CORCHORUS JAPONICUS, *or Double Japan Globe Flower.*

This shrub, although cultivated as a Green-house plant, will, nevertheless, thrive in the open garden. In the windows of a warm room, or in a Green-house, its slender branches are, during the months of March and April, bent down with the weight of its numerous flowers, of a golden yellow, which are produced in wreaths ; and there is scarcely a week, from spring to winter, that flowers may not be found on it, especially if it is planted during that season in the open ground, or continued there throughout the year.

HIBISCUS MUTABILIS, *or Chinese Changeable Hibiscus.*

This plant produces abundance of flowers during the months of November and December, which are about the size of a large garden Rose, and very beautiful. One great peculiarity which these flowers possess, is, that they change from white to a blush rose colour, and then to purple, which gives the plant an interesting appearance, from having flowers on it of different colours at the same time.

DATURA ARBOREA, or *Great Peruvian Datura.*

This plant, which is of vigorous growth, produces very splendid flowers during the months of October and November; they are pure white, of a pentangular form, with angular extensions, possess an agreeable fragrance, and are generally near a foot in length.

DAHLIA.

Of this beautiful plant, more than 150 varieties are now cultivated in Europe, 34 of which have double flowers. It is a native of Mexico, and the flowers are of every gradation, from the darkest lake colour to the lightest shades, and of every hue but green, and in splendour they are surpassed by those of no other plant.

The roots, which are tuberous, resemble a sweet potato, and can be taken up in the fall, and planted in boxes or pots until spring, when they can either be retained in the pots, or replanted along the borders of the garden; the latter situation is however preferable, as their growth is there so much more vigorous, and the flowers consequently more abundant. The end of April, or beginning of May, is the proper season for planting them out, when they will soon shoot up to the height of from five to eight feet, producing a great abundance of flowers, of which from thirty to forty are frequently in bloom on a single plant at the same time. The single flowering ones possess very vivid colours; but the double ones, from being the most rare and splendid, are the most esteemed—twenty-eight varieties of the latter are now in the possession of the proprietor, as will be seen by referring to page 102.

DIRECTIONS

FOR THE CULTURE OF BULBOUS AND FIBROUS FLOWER ROOTS.

Situation.

A southern aspect, dry and airy, and sheltered from the north winds, is preferable for most Bulbs, but Anemones and Ranunculuses will do best in a situation which, combining a southern aspect, is at the same time sheltered from the intense heat of a noonday sun.

Soil.

One third common sand, one third old well rotted cowyard manure, and one third good garden mould; let the beds thus formed be well pulverized to the depth of 15 or 18 inches, that the three component parts may be completely mixed together; a fourth part of rotten wood, or decomposed vegetable mould from a wood or swamp, if convenient to be had, may be added with advantage to the above, and will at all times be beneficial in giving additional lightness to the soil; and, when thus prepared, the soil need not be removed for five or six years. The beds should be raised four to six inches above the level of the walks, which will give an opportunity for all superfluous moisture to run off; some sand strewed in the trenches, both before and after placing the roots, would be of advantage.

Time of Planting.

For Hyacinths, Tulips, Crown Imperials, Lilies, Poleanthus Narcissus, Common Narcissus, Jonquils, Irises, Crocuses, Colchicums, Star of Bethlehem, Winter Aconites, Snowdrops, Snowflakes, Gladiolus, and most other hardy Bulbs, the preferable season for transplanting is the months of August, September, and October; and it would be well here to observe, that the above mentioned Bulbs will thrive best if not taken from the ground oftener than every second or third year.

The Ranunculus and Anemone are not so tender as is generally supposed; they may either be planted in October or November, in a warm situation, and be protected during winter by a covering of three or four inches of leaves or tanners' bark; or they may be kept in dry sand during the winter season, and be planted in March or April. To have a succession of flowers, a proportion may be planted in autumn, and the residue in the spring; and, if treated as above directed, very little care is necessary to have them flower in perfection.

The different species of Ferraria, Antholyza, Ixia, Crinum, and Hæmanthus, the tender kinds of Amaryllis, Pancratium, and Gladiolus, with most other delicate Bulbs, may be planted during the months of November or December, in pots, when intended to be sheltered during winter, or they can be kept in dry sand until the month of March or April, and then be planted in the open ground, when it has become free from frost, and perfectly settled.

Depths and Distances.

Hyacinths, Martagon, and other large Lilies and Pæonies, should be planted at a depth of four inches; Crown Imperials, and Poleanthus Narcissus, six inches; Tulips, Double and Single Narcissus, Jonquils, Colchicums, and Snowflakes, three inches; Bulbous Irises, Crocuses, Arums, small Fritillaries, Pancratium, Gladiolus, and Snowdrops, two inches; Ranunculuses, Anemones, and Dog's Tooth Violets, one inch; always measuring from the top of the Bulb. The rows should be about ten inches apart, and the roots be placed from four to six inches apart in the rows according to their size.

Protection during Winter.

On the approach of winter, it would be beneficial to cover the beds with tanners' bark, withered leaves, or light rotten earth from the woods, such as is formed by the decay of leaves, to the depth of two or three inches, as it prevents any ill effects which a very severe season might have on the roots; but it should be carefully raked off again early in the spring.

Taking up Bulbs after Blooming.

The only advantage to be gained by taking up Bulbs, is either to divide the roots when they have become too numerous, or to renew a worn out soil; neither of which can occur oftener than once in three years, and when they are taken up, it is preferable to plant them as soon as you have divided the roots, and prepared a fresh bed according to the directions already given.

About a month after the bloom is passed, the foliage puts on a yellow decayed appearance; this is the proper season for taking them up; on doing which, you must cut off the stem and foliage within an inch of the Bulb, leaving the fibrous roots attached to it. After thus preparing them, they must be spread singly in an airy room for two or three weeks to dry; and then each root must be wrapped carefully in paper, or put in dry sand until replanted.

Hyacinths, and other Bulbs, to bloom in pots or glasses.

For this purpose, single Hyacinths, and such as are designated as earliest among the double, are to be preferred.—Double and single Jonquils, Poleanthus Narcissus, and double Narcissus, also make a fine appearance during the winter season.

Bulbs intended for blooming in pots during the winter season, should be planted during the months of October and November, and be left exposed to the open air until it begins to freeze, and then be placed in the Green-house, or a warm room. They will need moderate occasional waterings, and should be exposed as much as possible to the sun and light, to prevent the leaves from growing too long, or becoming yellow.

Those intended for glasses should be placed in them about the middle of November, the glasses being previously filled with pure water, so that the bottom of the Bulb may touch the water, then place them for the first ten days in a dark room, to promote the shooting of the roots, after which expose them to the light and sun as much as possible; the water should be changed as often as it becomes impure, and care be taken not to suffer it to freeze.

REMARKS.

TULIP—*Tulipa gesneriana.*

In no class of plants has nature so varied her delicate tints as in this; it would seem as if each change which nature or art is capable of forming, was included in the varying beauties of the Tulip, above 1,100 varieties of which are cultivated in some of the gardens of Holland. All the finer varieties, however, of this delightful flower, have been obtained, by cultivation and art, during the last two centuries, through the perseverance of the Dutch, French, and Flemish florists; several kinds of which possess a delightful fragrance, although persons who are ignorant of this circumstance, have made the want of it an objection to this splendid flower.— About the middle of the seventeenth century the rage for this flower was so great in Holland, that from four to twenty-five thousand florins were given for a single root. The Tulip called *Semper Augustus* was sold for ten thousand florins, ($ 4,000,) and the one called *Viceroi*, for twenty-five thousand florins, ($ 10,000.) This extraordinary traffic was, however, soon checked by the interference of the Legislature, who enacted that no Tulip, or other flower, should be in future sold for a sum exceeding about fifty guineas; and so effectual has been this law, that at present the highest price of any Tulip in that country is only one hundred and fifty florins, ($ 60,) and the highest priced Lily three hundred florins, ($ 120.) Tulips are divided into early and late blowers; the former begin blooming about the 15th of April, and are followed by the later kinds in succession until the end of May; the late kinds produce the largest flowers, the stems of which are generally from twenty to thirty inches in height.

HYACINTHS—*Hyacinthus orientalis.*

This favourite flower, which, with its great beauty, combines also the most exquisite fragrance, has been cultivated in Holland to an equal extent with the Tulip, and 1,300 varieties are found in the gardens of that country. The first double Hyacinth known in Holland was raised from seed about the end of the seventeenth century, by Peter Voorhelm, from which all the fine double varieties we now possess may be traced. So great was the value of a fine double Hyacinth formerly in Holland, that from two to ten thousand florins were given for a single root; and Mr. Dutens mentions, that, in his travels in that country, 1771, he saw ten thousaud florins ($ 4,000) refused for a single Bulb. So extensive has their cultivation, however, now become, that many acres are occupied by individuals solely for that purpose, and many hundred thousand roots are annually exported to other countries; and the prices have been so reduced, that no Hyacinths are now sold at more than one hundred florins each, and few higher than from two to five guineas, and by far the greater number at much less rates. Single Hyacinths are held in less estimation than double ones; their colours, however, are more vivid, and their bells, though smaller, are more numerous; they are preferable for flowering in winter to most of the double ones, as they bloom two or three weeks earlier.

It has been supposed by many that Hyacinths, Tulips, and other Bulbous Flowers, are difficult of culture, and that our country being unfavourable to their growth, they would dwindle and decline after a few years' cultivation. This is altogether a mistaken impression; and, if it ever occurs, must be owing to improper treatment, as no country in the world possesses a climate more congenial to the culture of Bulbous Flowers than the middle states; for the disadvantages of great fogs and a humid atmosphere, which are so much complained of by the Dutch as appertaining to their climate, do not at all exist in our's. The great ascendency which Holland has ever held in the culture of Bulbous Flowers, is the result of its soil, which is of peculiar formation, being a combination of marine sand made fresh by cultivation and bog mould; the proper means, therefore, to succeed equally in their culture, is to form a soil as near as possible of the same component parts, which is by no means a difficult task. And, in fact, after all that has been said and written on the particular cultivation of Bulbous Roots, we often see the finest flowers in gardens where little or no attention is paid to them; and, perhaps, there is no class of plants which affords us so many delights, and so richly repays us for each little care bestowed on them.

It is intended to add annually to the collection of Bulbous Flowers, by importations from the most celebrated gardens in Holland; and, indeed, since the previous part of this Catalogue was put to press, above 8,000 roots have been received; among which are several hundred varieties not included in this Catalogue, some of which cost from ten to twenty guilders each. It may be well to remark, that the Bulbs which are frequently sent out on consignment to this country from Holland, and sold at our auctions, are the mere refuse, and such as are held in no esteem, either by amateurs or connoisseurs, and no idea can be formed by them of the beauty of the more estimable kinds ; and it is to be regretted that our citizens should have been so often duped in their purchases of these roots, under the imposition of high sounding names.

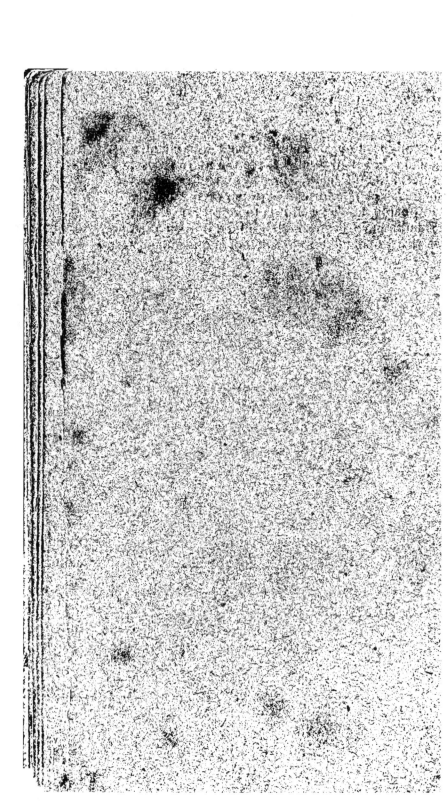

CPSIA information can be obtained
at www.ICGtesting.com
Printed in the USA
BVHW041124150119
537879BV00009B/285/P